SMART STARTUPS

GUIDANCE FROM 18 HARVARD BUSINESS ICONS

SAGE THOMPSON

Copyright © 2024 by Sage Thompson

All rights reserved.

No part of this publication may be reproduced, distributed, or transmitted in any form or by any means, including photocopying, recording, or other electronic or mechanical methods, without the prior written permission of the publisher, except in the case of brief quotations embodied in critical reviews and certain other noncommercial uses permitted by copyright law.

The information in this book is true and complete to the best of our knowledge. All recommendations are made without guarantee on the part of the author or publisher. The author and publisher disclaim any liability in connection with the use of information

Table of contents

INTRODUCTION   7
    Welcome to Smart Startups!   7
    Why Harvard Business Icons?   9
    Utilizing This Book   12

CHAPTER 1   17
THE STARTUP MENTALITY   17
    Accepting the Spirit of Entrepreneurship   17
    The Impact of HBS: Fostering Leadership   20
    Mindset Above Matter: Adaptability and Resilience 24

CHAPTER 2   31
DISCOVERING YOUR SPECIALTY   31
    Finding Gaps in the Market   31
    Making Use of Harvard Networks   34
    Case Study: [Founder 1] and Their Distinctive Place in the Market   37

CHAPTER 3   45
FORMULATING A ROBUST BUSINESS STRATEGY 45
    Crucial Elements of an Enterprise Strategy   45
    Harvard Methods for Successful Planning   51
    Case Study: [Founder 2] and Their Business Blueprint   54

CHAPTER 4   63
GETTING FUNDS FOR YOUR STARTUP   63
    Comprehending Various Funding Choices   63
    Attracting Capitalists: HBS Perspectives   68
    Case Study: [Founder 3] and Their Funding Journey 71

CHAPTER 5 — 79
PUTTING TOGETHER YOUR IDEAL GROUP — 79
- Team Dynamics' Significance — 79
- Harvard Employment Practices — 82
- Case Study: [Founder 4] and Their Achievements in Team Building — 86

CHAPTER 6 — 93
INNOVATION AND PRODUCT DEVELOPMENT — 93
- The Development Process: From Idea to Market — 93
- Innovation: Staying on the Cutting Edge — 98
- Case Study: [Founder 5] and Their Innovative Approach — 101

CHAPTER 7 — 109
MARKETING AND BRANDING — 109
- Developing an Engaging Brand Narrative — 109
- Harvard Methods for Successful Marketing — 113
- Case Study: [Founder 6] and Their Branding Success — 116

CHAPTER 8 — 125
EXPANDING YOUR COMPANY — 125
- Techniques for Long-Term Development — 125
- Overcoming Difficulties in Scaling — 129
- Case Study: [Founder 7] and Their Growth Journey — 133

CHAPTER 9 — 141
OVERCOMING OBSTACLES AND SETBACKS — 141
- Typical Startup Errors and Solutions — 141
- Failure-Related Lessons: HBS Views — 146
- Case Study: [Founder 8] and Their Turnaround Story

149

CHAPTER 10   **159**
TECHNOLOGY'S FUNCTION IN STARTUPS   **159**
    Using Technology to Gain a Competitive Edge   159
    Harvard Perspectives on Technology Inclusion   163
    Case Study: [Founder 9] and Their Tech-Driven Success   166

CHAPTER 11   **175**
THE VIEW FROM A GLOBAL ANGLE   **175**
    Extending Across Boundaries   175
    Harvard Techniques for Global Marketplaces   180
    Case Study: [Founder 10] and Their Global Expansion   184

CHAPTER 12   **193**
MORAL BUSINESS PRACTICES   **193**
    The Value of Morality in Business   193
    Harvard's Social Responsibility Philosophy   195
    Case Study: [Founder 11] and Their Ethical Business Model   197

CHAPTER 13   **207**
LONG-TERM GOALS AND STRATEGIES FOR LIVING   **207**
    Future Planning: Scaling or Selling   207
    Harvard Views on Profitable Exits   210
    Case Study: [Founder 12] and Their Exit Strategy   214

CHAPTER 14   **223**
BALANCING WORK AND LIFE   **223**
    Achieving Harmony Between Work and Life   223

Harvard Advice on Keeping Your Balance	226
Case Study: [Founder 13] and Their Approach to Work-Life Balance	229

CHAPTER 15 — 237
CONTINUOUS LEARNING AND ADAPTATION — 237

The Importance of Lifelong Learning	237
Harvard's Culture of Continuous Improvement	239
Case Study: [Founder 14] and Their Learning Journey	242

CHAPTER 16 — 251
CREATING A LEGACY — 251

Thinking Beyond Profits	251
Harvard Perspectives on Making a Permanent Impression	253
Case Study: [Founder 15] and Their Legacy	256

CHAPTER 17 — 265
GUIDANCE FOR FUTURE BUSINESS OWNERS — 265

Harvard Business Icons: Crucial Lessons	265
Useful Advice for Beginning Your Trip	269
Inspirational Quotes from All 18 Founders	273

CHAPTER 18 — 279
CONCLUSIONS AND PROSPECTS — 279

The Future of Startups: What's Next?	279
Harvard Entrepreneurship Predictions	284
Authors' Concluding Remarks	288

CONCLUSION — 295

Summary of Important Lessons	295
Motivation for Your Business Adventure	304

INTRODUCTION

Welcome to Smart Startups!

Imagine yourself at the starting point of an exciting adventure, poised to explore new ground. As your reliable guide, Smart Startups: Advice from 18 Harvard Business Icons is a well-worn road map that shows you the way to success and is based on the knowledge and experiences of those who have gone before you.

Greetings from the world of startups, where ideas become reality, dreams come true, and there are always fresh opportunities and challenges to be faced. This book is meant to be your road map, providing priceless ideas from some of the most brilliant people in the business world, whether you're an experienced founder seeking to improve your approach or an ambitious entrepreneur with a game-changing concept.

Harvard Business School (HBS), a name linked with leadership, innovation, and quality, is where our adventure starts. It's where some of the most successful businesspeople in the world have developed their abilities, tried out their concepts, and started their enterprises. You will meet eighteen of these Harvard Business legends in this book who have kindly offered their experiences, tactics, and takeaways from their successful careers.

However, this book is more than simply a compilation of tips; it's a story of successes and failures, innovations and disappointments, all interwoven to provide a wealth of entrepreneurial knowledge. You will discover the inner workings of successful businesses, the strategic thinking that propels them, and the human tales that make these teachings come to life as you read through these pages.

Why Harvard Business Icons?

Why are Harvard Business Icons' insights so valuable? Let's step back and examine what Harvard Business School stands for in order to respond to this issue. HBS, which was founded in 1908, has served as a testing ground for innovation and leadership, molding a number of business executives who have gone on to have a major influence on a variety of global businesses. Academic achievement and practical, real-world success are fostered in an atmosphere that is unmatched by the demanding curriculum, elite faculty, and unmatched network.

This also applies to the entrepreneurs in this book. Their backgrounds are varied, and they work in a variety of sectors, including consumer products, healthcare, technology, and finance. Their mutual conviction in the efficacy of strategic thinking, resilience, and ongoing education, as well as their HBS experiences, are what bind them together.

The same difficulties that plague all entrepreneurs have been encountered by their founders: little resources, intense rivalry, and an ongoing push to innovate. Nevertheless, they have not only survived but also prospered, founding companies that have upended markets, spurred notable expansion, and, often, completely changed sectors.

These Harvard business giants provide a special synthesis of academic understanding and real-world application by sharing their personal tales. They provide a glimpse into effective tactics, potential hazards, and the mentality required to successfully negotiate the challenging landscape of startups. Their perspectives are not only theoretical; they have been tried and true, having been refined in the furnace of practical experience.

You will learn the value of a strong business strategy, the subtleties of assembling and managing a team, the complexities of obtaining finance, and the skill of growing a company as you read through their stories. What's maybe even more significant is that you'll discover the human aspect of entrepreneurship—the drive, tenacity, and personal development that are just as much a part of the process as any business plan.

Utilizing This Book

Consider this book to be a mentor as well as a guide, giving you the freedom to customize your reading experience to suit your own requirements. Here are some tips to help you maximize it:

Sequential Reading: If you're unfamiliar with the startup industry, you may want to read the whole book. The chapters are structured to flow logically from the core ideas of the startup mentality through the several phases of creating and growing a company. With each chapter building on the knowledge from the preceding one, this strategy will provide you with a thorough comprehension of the entrepreneurial path.

Targeted Learning: Feel free to skip to the chapters that are most relevant to your requirements if you are an experienced entrepreneur or if you are encountering certain issues. Every chapter offers in-depth analyses of certain subjects, including fundraising, team building, product development, and marketing, and is designed to stand alone. To go straight to the sections where you want the most assistance, use the Table of Contents.

Case Studies and Practical Examples: The 18 highlighted Harvard Business icons are the source of case studies and examples found throughout the book. These true tales provide specific instances of how the concepts and tactics covered have been effectively implemented, illuminating the underlying ideas. These case studies are very informative and inspiring; pay special attention to them.

Actionable Insights: Each chapter concludes with a set of actionable actions and key takeaways that condense the most significant lessons into doable recommendations. These action steps are intended to assist you in putting what you've learned into practice in your own company, whether it's improving your leadership abilities, honing your business plan, or creating a fresh marketing strategy.

Adaptation and Reflection: While reading, consider how the tips and techniques you've been given relate to your own struggles and experiences. Since being an entrepreneur is not a one-size-fits-all experience, it is essential to be able to modify and customize these insights to meet your unique situation. When you read, think about journaling or taking notes to record your ideas, goals, and reflections on how you may apply these lessons to your company.

Make Use of the Resources: The appendices provide further tools, resources, and references to help you on your entrepreneurial path. These resources, which range from suggested readings to useful tools and templates, are meant to supplement the knowledge gained from the book and provide additional direction as you go.

Smart Startups: Advice from 18 Harvard Business Icons is a toolset, a roadmap, and an inspiration source in addition to being a book. It's evidence of the value of studying people who have gone before you and using their insights to better navigate your own business journey.

Keep in mind that every startup journey is distinct and comes with a unique set of chances and obstacles as you begin out on your trip. These Harvard Business symbols provide tactics and insights that are meant to be guiding principles rather than prescriptions that you may modify to suit your objectives and vision.

Greetings on this once-in-a-lifetime excursion. You have access to the knowledge of some of the top business minds when you use this book as a guide. Allow their tales to uplift you, their wisdom to direct you, and their accomplishments to spur you on to achieve your business goals with self-assurance and tenacity.

Now let's get going.

CHAPTER 1

THE STARTUP MENTALITY

Accepting the Spirit of Entrepreneurship

Picture yourself at the boundary of a huge, unexplored wilderness. There is a vast horizon in front of you that is full of uncharted territory, undiscovered prospects, and boundless potential for profit. This is the realm of business; it's a journey that calls for both an unwavering attitude and a daring vision. Adopting an entrepreneurial mindset entails plunging headfirst into this uncharted territory with curiosity, adventure, and unwavering determination.

Let's put ourselves in Sarah's shoes. She just graduated from Harvard Business School and wanted to launch her own business because she was driven by her love of technology and her desire to make the world a better place. Sarah's journey starts in the HBS lecture halls, where she is motivated by the tales of successful business owners who have occupied the same seats and dealt with the same concerns and anxieties. She discovered that being an entrepreneur involves more than simply launching a company; it also entails identifying opportunities where others see barriers, bringing ideas to life, and bringing about change with a strong sense of purpose.

Mark, an HBS alumni who started a profitable fintech business, was one of her main sources of motivation. Mark's tale was especially interesting as, after several setbacks, he eventually struck gold by creating a platform that completely changed internet lending. Sarah found it remarkable that Mark remained steadfast in his pursuit of his goal in the face of obstacles. Instead of seeing each setback as a loss, he saw them as learning opportunities that allowed him to improve his strategy.

Sarah took this lesson to heart. Accepting that failure is a necessary part of the path means embracing the entrepreneurial spirit. It's about keeping a good mindset, being driven, and always looking for methods to do better. It involves having the guts to take chances, the tenacity to go on through hardship, and the fortitude to overcome disappointments.

But it was an insight Sarah gained during a late-night brainstorming session with her classmates that really sparked her entrepreneurial spirit. They were talking about possible ways to increase underdeveloped nations' access to clean water. Sarah felt a rush of excitement and energy as ideas were discussed and bounced around the room. She came to the realization that this was the core of entrepreneurship: the excitement of inventing something new, the delight of finding solutions to important issues, and the fulfillment of changing the world for the better.

The Impact of HBS: Fostering Leadership

Harvard Business School is a testing ground for leadership and innovation development, not merely a school of higher learning. The goal of the HBS atmosphere is to push students beyond their comfort zones, challenge them, and better prepare them for the intricacies of the business world. Sarah's time at HBS changed her life and made her a leader prepared to face the world of entrepreneurship.

HBS places a strong emphasis on leadership from the outset. The curriculum is demanding, with case studies that put students in the position of company executives having to make important choices. These examples expose students to a broad variety of situations and issues across sectors and geographical locations. These activities helped Sarah greatly in refining her strategic thinking and decision-making abilities.

Sarah found great resonance in a case study that told the tale of a healthcare business that encountered a significant moral conundrum. The creators had to choose between putting patient safety and commercial margins first. Students were forced to think about the ethical aspects of this case in addition to the commercial consequences since it generated intense arguments in the classroom. Through these conversations, Sarah discovered that genuine leadership entails weighing the interests of many stakeholders, making difficult choices under duress, and consistently attempting to do what is right.

However, HBS has an impact beyond academia. Students are encouraged to learn from each other's experiences and viewpoints in the school's collaborative atmosphere. Sarah became close to her classmates, many of whom had distinguished careers in a variety of fields. Through these connections, she was able to access a variety of perspectives and a network of support that deepened her knowledge of leadership and business.

David, an HBS professor and serial entrepreneur renowned for his engaging teaching style and practical insight, was one of Sarah's mentors. David underlined the need for emotional intelligence and self-awareness in leadership. "Leadership is not just about making the right decisions; it's about inspiring others, building trust, and creating a vision that people want to follow," he would often remind his pupils.

Sarah was greatly impacted by David's mentoring. She discovered that developing one's leadership requires constant introspection, learning new things, and personal development. It's about realizing your advantages and disadvantages, being receptive to criticism, and never stopping the pursuit of improvement.

Furthermore, HBS gives its students a feeling of accountability. The goal of the school is to produce leaders who have an impact on society. This philosophy encouraged Sarah to look at the bigger picture of her business ventures rather than just the immediate financial gain. She came to see that, in her capacity as a leader, she could effect constructive change and make significant contributions to society.

Mindset Above Matter: Adaptability and Resilience

The only thing that is consistent in the startup industry is change. Success requires the capacity to adjust to changing conditions, change course when called for, and persevere in the face of difficulty. This lesson was evident to Sarah in the early phases of her entrepreneurial experience.

Sarah started a digital company after graduating from HBS with the goal of giving underprivileged areas access to reasonably priced and environmentally friendly energy solutions. Sarah and her colleagues were optimistic because of the early reaction, which seemed positive. But as they started to grow, they ran into unanticipated difficulties, including supply chain hiccups, regulatory obstacles, and fierce rivalry.

These challenges put Sarah's fortitude to the test. There were times when giving up looked like the simpler course of action, along with periods of uncertainty and irritation. However, Sarah found solace in the knowledge she had gained during her time at HBS and in the accounts of other business owners who had endured such hardships. She recalled Mark's tale and his capacity to see setbacks as teaching moments.

Sarah came to the realization that resilience is about how you handle failure rather than trying to prevent it. It all comes down to keeping a development mentality, which views obstacles as chances to improve and learn. Sarah and her group stepped back, reviewed their plan, and made the required modifications. They improved their business plan, looked for new alliances, and created cutting-edge products.

Choosing to concentrate on a specialized market that bigger rivals had ignored was one of Sarah's team's biggest turns. Although this development necessitated a significant adjustment to their strategy, it created fresh chances and laid the groundwork for their ultimate success. Sarah learned from this experience that resilience requires adaptation in order to function. Startups are able to survive and thrive in the uncertain world of entrepreneurship because they have the flexibility to pivot, experiment, and iterate.

Taking care of oneself and one's team members is another aspect of resilience. Running a business may be very stressful, and burnout is a genuine possibility. Establishing a culture of support and inclusivity among her staff was a top concern for Sarah. She made sure that everyone felt appreciated and inspired, promoted open communication, and acknowledged little victories.

Sarah also looked for counselors and mentors who might provide direction and encouragement. Lisa, an accomplished businesswoman and HBS alumni who had skillfully weathered the ups and downs of the startup sector, served as one of her mentors. Lisa provided both strategic insights and emotional support in her counsel, which was priceless. She emphasized to Sarah that developing a network of support and making use of the combined knowledge of individuals in your immediate vicinity are equally important components of resilience, in addition to personal strength.

Sarah considered her path so far as her business started to take off. Her development of an entrepreneurial attitude, which included embracing innovation, honing leadership abilities, and fortifying resilience, had been crucial to her success in overcoming obstacles.

Final Thoughts

The cornerstone of every successful business journey is a startup mentality. It's about adopting an adventurous, inquisitive, and unwavering attitude of drive. It involves developing leadership abilities that uplift and mentor others while striking a balance between morality and strategic thinking. It also involves being resilient and adaptive and seeing setbacks as chances to improve.

For Sarah, a road map for navigating the challenging and sometimes unexpected world of startups came from the skills she acquired at Harvard Business School and the experiences of other accomplished business owners. When starting your own business, keep in mind that having the correct attitude may make all the difference. Accept the difficulties, hold on to your goals, and develop the fortitude necessary to overcome setbacks and prosper in the face of difficulty.

You will experience both highs and lows, victories and losses, along your business journey. However, you may overcome these obstacles and realize your goal if you have the correct mentality. Embrace the adventure with an entrepreneurial spirit, and allow your enthusiasm and tenacity to propel you towards success. Welcome to the world of startups.

CHAPTER 2

DISCOVERING YOUR SPECIALTY

Finding Gaps in the Market

In the congested startup scene, finding your specialty may often seem like trying to find a needle in a haystack. But it's a crucial phase that may determine how your business develops. Finding market gaps—those unmet demands or neglected markets that provide chances for innovation and expansion—is the first step in the process.

Consider yourself Sam is a recent graduate of Harvard Business School who is passionate about sustainability. Sam and his group were assigned to create a business plan for a new product as part of a class assignment. When they dug further into market research, they saw a pattern: although many businesses were concentrating on green energy, very few were tackling the inefficiencies in residential water consumption.

Something aroused Sam's interest. He started looking into it further, interviewing and surveying customers to learn about their problems. He found that while a lot of individuals wanted to lessen their water footprint, they were lacking the knowledge and resources necessary to do it successfully. This realization exposed a major vacuum in the market: there was a need for reasonably priced, approachable water monitoring and use solutions for homes.

Finding this gap was just the first step. Sam understood he had to go farther in order to make this notion a workable company. He examined rivals, examined market trends, and estimated the market's prospective size. He discovered that the market for water conservation was expanding and that the current, often costly, and complex solutions were underserving the needs of the industry.

Sam took the next step after seeing the gap in the market: creating a solution to bridge this gap. His idea was for a simple-to-install smart water management system that would provide real-time statistics on water consumption along with conservation advice. He thought that this device may enable users to manage their water use and support sustainability.

Sam built a prototype and tested it on a group of early adopters in order to confirm his concept. The vast majority of responses were favorable, with users praising the system's ease of use and efficiency. Inspired by this feedback, Sam improved the product and started organizing a wider release.

Making Use of Harvard Networks

The ability to connect with a large and powerful network is one of the biggest benefits of graduating from HBS. Making the most of these relationships may provide priceless chances, insights, and support that can help your business succeed. For Sam, the Harvard network was essential to transforming his concept into a profitable business.

Sam started by reaching out to the HBS alumni community. He made contact with instructors and previous students who were knowledgeable in technology and sustainability. He received insightful criticism from these discussions, which enabled him to improve his company plan. Professor Thompson, one of his mentors, was very helpful. Thompson, who has years of expertise in environmental technology, provided helpful guidance on developing new products and entering new markets.

Sam was able to contact possible investors via the Harvard network. Sam presented his proposal to a group of venture investors at an alumni gathering. Lisa, an HBS alumni who had made successful investments in a number of green tech businesses, was one of them. Sam's vision and the depth of his market study astonished her. Following many conversations, Lisa consented to spearhead an initial investment round, furnishing Sam with the monetary support he required to expand his business.

However, the Harvard network's assistance didn't end there. Sam also made use of the resources made accessible by the several programs and institutes at HBS. For instance, he had access to state-of-the-art technology, a workspace, and experienced entrepreneurs as mentors at the Harvard Innovation Labs. Sam was able to interact with possible partners and clients and improve his go-to-market strategy with the aid of the i-Lab's accelerator program.

With these contacts, Sam was able to assemble a formidable advisory board. This team of professionals opened doors to strategic alliances and offered continuing advice. Sam's market reach was further increased when he partnered with a top smart home technology firm, which included his water management system in its product line.

Case Study: [Founder 1] and Their Distinctive Place in the Market

Let's examine the tale of another recent HBS alumnus who identified and profited from a distinctive market niche. Introducing Emily, the creator of EcoThreads, a business transforming the fashion industry by producing clothes that are ethically and sustainably made.

Emily's path started because of a personal annoyance. She was a passionate fashion fan who had trouble finding chic, reasonably priced apparel that complemented her beliefs about ethical and sustainable manufacturing. She found that most eco-friendly goods were either too pricey or didn't have the desired visual appeal. Emily saw that there was a big gap in the market: she and other customers desired stylish, reasonably priced, and environmentally friendly clothes, but there weren't many possibilities.

Emily used this realization to launch a brand that would close this gap. She began by gathering a lot of information about the market, interviewing prospective clients, and researching market trends. She found that rising consumer knowledge of environmental concerns was driving a sharp increase in demand for sustainable fashion. But a lot of businesses weren't successfully able to satisfy this desire.

The next task for Emily was to create a distinctive value proposition that would make EcoThreads stand out from its competitors. She made the decision to concentrate on three main factors: cost, style, and sustainability. She connected with ethical producers and acquired eco-friendly products to assure sustainability.

She used a direct-to-consumer business strategy and reduced her supply chain to keep costs down. Additionally, she worked with emerging fashion designers who shared her vision to guarantee the style of her products.

Emily started EcoThreads with a distinct market position. Her marketing approach centered on informing customers about how fashion affects the environment and emphasizing the advantages of her goods. She developed a devoted clientele by using content marketing, influencer relationships, and social media.

EcoThreads took off right away. Customers valued the brand's honest business procedures, and those with an ethical conscience were drawn to the affordable, stylish, and sustainable offerings. Because of her distinct market position, Emily was able to stand out in a crowded field and develop a devoted fan base.

Getting a mention in a big fashion magazine via Emily's Harvard network was one of the turning moments for EcoThreads. She got the brand discovered by key editors with the support of another HBS alumnus who works in the media. Sales and brand awareness increased as a consequence of the increased exposure and credibility that the publicity brought about for EcoThreads.

Emily stayed true to her principles even as EcoThreads expanded. She created new product lines while adhering to rigorous environmental guidelines and using strategic alliances to investigate untapped markets. EcoThreads has established itself as a pioneer in sustainable fashion because of her ability to spot market gaps and develop distinctive value propositions.

Final Thoughts

Identifying your specialization is a crucial first step for every firm. It requires careful observation, in-depth study, and a profound comprehension of market dynamics. Finding market gaps enables you to find underserved markets and unmet demands, which opens up possibilities for uniqueness and innovation.

Making use of networks—particularly ones as strong as the Harvard Business School community—can provide priceless resources and assistance. Having relationships with investors, mentors, and business leaders may help you overcome obstacles when founding and growing your firm.

The success of securing a distinctive market position is shown by the tales of Sam and Emily. They were successful in creating enterprises that had an effect because they were able to discover holes in the market and design solutions that met particular requirements. Their experiences show how crucial it is to stick to your goals, make the most of your network, and constantly adjust to the needs of the market.

Remember these tales as you set out on your own business path. Seek out market gaps, pay attention to what customers need, and be ready to innovate and adjust. Use your networks to your advantage to get opportunities, assistance, and insights. Above all, don't waver from your vision and core principles as you carve out a distinct niche for your business.

Greetings from the fascinating realm of identifying your specialty. You can transform market gaps into opportunities and create a business that not only succeeds but also has a significant effect if you have the correct strategy and mentality.

44

CHAPTER 3

FORMULATING A ROBUST BUSINESS STRATEGY

Crucial Elements of an Enterprise Strategy

An excellent business plan serves as your startup's roadmap. It describes your objectives, your vision, and a plan of action for reaching them. Several essential elements go into crafting a successful business plan, all of which are necessary to provide a solid basis for your endeavor. Let's examine these elements by following the path taken by Alex, a recent graduate of Harvard Business School who founded a profitable edtech company.

Executive Summary: Although it is the first component of your business plan, it is often written last. It gives a succinct synopsis of your company that includes your mission statement, the issue you're trying to solve, your proposed solution, and your objectives. In his executive summary, Alex outlined his goal of transforming online education by offering individualized and interesting learning opportunities. He gave a quick overview of his ground-breaking platform, which leverages AI to customize material to each learner's unique learning style, and he laid out his audacious plans for expanding his user base and gaining market share.

industry analysis: Finding possibilities and strategically positioning your startup depend on your ability to comprehend the state of the industry. Alex carried out a thorough analysis of the market to determine target demographics, evaluate the competitive environment, and examine the edtech sector. The expanding need for online education, the drawbacks of the available options, and the possibility of disruption were all covered in depth in his market analysis section. He demonstrated a thorough grasp of market dynamics and trends by using facts and statistics to back up his conclusions.

Company Description: Your company's history, organizational structure, and basic beliefs are all covered in detail in this area. Alex gave a description of how his dissatisfaction with conventional teaching techniques led to the founding of his firm, EduSmart. He outlined the organization's structure, outlining the duties of important team members, and underlined EduSmart's dedication to high-quality instruction and accessibility.

Products and Services: Describe the goods and services your startup provides in this section. Alex gave a thorough rundown of the EduSmart platform, emphasizing its special qualities and advantages. He described how the platform provides students with real-time feedback, dynamic and interesting information, and individualized learning routes created by sophisticated algorithms. Future plans to add more topics and sophisticated analytics to the platform's services were also described by Alex.

Marketing and Sales Strategy: This part describes your approach to bringing in and keeping clients. In order to raise brand recognition and promote user acquisition, Alex's marketing approach made use of influencer relationships, digital media, and alliances with academic institutions. He described his sales process in depth, from lead generation to conversion, and stressed the need to keep customers engaged and supported throughout time.

Operations Plan: This document outlines the daily tasks necessary to maintain your company. Alex gave a rundown of the EduSmart operational procedures, including data analytics, client assistance, platform upkeep, and content production. He outlined the resources and technologies required to reach each major milestone, along with a schedule for doing so.

Management staff: confident and experienced staff is what investors look for when making an investment. Alex gave a brief introduction of his co-founders and important team members, stressing their experiences, qualifications, and accomplishments for the firm. He highlighted his team's complimentary abilities and their combined background in technology, business management, and education.

Financial Plan: Revenue, spending, and profitability estimates are included in the financial plan. In-depth balance sheets, cash flow statements, and income statements were all given by Alex. He described his needs for money and how he planned to utilize it to further his company's objectives. Alex provided anticipated growth rates and a break-even analysis as well, showing a direct route to profitability.

Appendix: Supporting documentation and other details are included in this appendix. In this area, Alex provided screenshots of the product, client testimonials, legal papers, and statistics from market research.

Harvard Methods for Successful Planning

Not only does one need information, but also strategic thinking and practical insights to create a strong company strategy. Students at Harvard Business School are better prepared to plan thanks to a variety of frameworks and methodologies. Alex used the following Harvard tactics in his business plan:

SWOT Analysis: A SWOT analysis assists in determining the opportunities, threats, weaknesses, and strengths of your startup. Alex evaluated EduSmart's external environment and internal capabilities using this approach. He saw potential in the expanding edtech business, risks from well-established rivals, and drawbacks, including limited early capital and a strong team. Alex was able to create plans to take advantage of chances, minimize vulnerabilities, counter threats, and play to his strengths because of this study.

Porter's Five Forces: An industry's competitive forces are examined using this framework. In order to comprehend the competitive dynamics of the edtech sector, Alex utilized Porter's Five Forces. He assessed the strength of the competition, the danger of substitutes and new competitors, and the negotiating power of suppliers and purchasers. His ideas for setting EduSmart apart from rivals and creating long-lasting competitive advantages were shaped by this insight.

Balanced Scorecard: This instrument for strategic planning aids in converting strategy and vision into attainable objectives. Alex created a balanced set of goals from four angles using this tool: learning and development, internal procedures, customers, and finances. By using this strategy, EduSmart was able to guarantee that its business plan was thorough and in line with its long-term goals.

Lean Startup Approach: Iterative development, verified learning, and quick experimentation are the main focuses of the Lean Startup approach. Alex used this strategy to create and improve the EduSmart platform. In order to make ongoing changes, he tested his minimum viable product (MVP) on a small group of early adopters and collected their comments. Through this iterative approach, Alex was able to improve the value proposition of the platform, lower risks, and confirm his assumptions.

Value Proposition Canvas: This tool assists new businesses in matching consumer demands with their offerings. Alex studied EduSmart's target market, their problems, and how his platform might solve them using the Value Proposition Canvas. Through customer segmentation and value proposition mapping, Alex made sure that EduSmart's solutions were appealing, unique, and relevant.

Case Study: [Founder 2] and Their Business Blueprint

Let's examine the tale of John, a fellow HBS alumnus who established GreenTech Solutions, a company dedicated to creating sustainable energy solutions for urban settings, in order to highlight the need for a strong business strategy. John started out wanting to stop climate change and had a strong enthusiasm for renewable energy. He was motivated by the idea that clean technology might turn cities into sustainable powerhouses when he was an undergraduate at

Harvard Business School. He was aware of the difficulties, too, including market fragmentation, regulatory obstacles, and exorbitant expenses.

John started with a clear idea in mind and wrote a business plan to see GreenTech Solutions through to success. He began with the fundamentals and painstakingly crafted each segment to demonstrate his strategic thinking and in-depth knowledge of the industry.

Executive Summary: John's summary effectively encapsulated the goal of GreenTech Solutions, which is to provide reasonably priced and effective renewable energy options for cities. He described the issue of inefficient use of energy in cities and presented his novel solution, which consisted of solar panels that could be readily incorporated into the current infrastructure. John outlined his objectives, which include lowering carbon emissions and providing sustainable energy to every city dweller.

Market Analysis: To pinpoint important developments and openings in the renewable energy industry, John carried out in-depth market research. He examined the possibility for creative solutions, the difficulties encountered by conventional energy suppliers, and the rising demand for clean energy in urban areas. John demonstrated his in-depth knowledge of the market by providing a thorough study of the competitive environment, regulatory frameworks, and patterns of energy usage.

Company Description: John gave a thorough rundown of GreenTech Solutions' goals, values, and purpose in this section. He outlined the company's distinct strategy for using renewable energy, stressing its emphasis on cost, innovation, and sustainability. John also described the ownership, location, and legal makeup of the business.

Products and Services: John described the main offering from GreenTech Solutions, which are solar panels that are modular and intended for urban settings. He described how the panels could be quickly and simply mounted on walls, roofs, and other buildings to provide dependable and efficient energy. John spoke about plans for future product development while highlighting the device's distinctive characteristics, which include real-time monitoring and superior energy storage.

Marketing and Sales Strategy: John positioned GreenTech Solutions as a leader in the urban energy sector and worked to increase public knowledge of the advantages of renewable energy. He described his strategies for public relations, internet marketing, and collaborations with local authorities and environmental groups. John also went into depth about his approach to sales, which included working with utility providers, forming alliances with real estate developers, and making direct sales to customers.

Operations Plan: John sent over a comprehensive plan that included the steps and materials required to manufacture, install, and maintain the solar panels. He went over the production procedures, quality control procedures, and supply chain. John also provided a schedule of important dates for things like new product development, market growth, and product introduction.

Management Team: John highlighted the engineering, business management, and renewable energy backgrounds of his co-founders and important team members. He highlighted the group's combined expertise and enthusiasm for sustainability. John also spoke about the advisory board, which was made up of mentors and industry professionals who offered assistance and direction in terms of strategy.

Financial Plan: John provided specific estimates for his earnings, costs, and profitability. Financial statements comprising cash flow, balance sheet, and income statements were submitted by him. John also described his needs for cash and how he planned to utilize it to further his company objectives. He provided expected growth rates and a break-even analysis, showing a direct route to profitability.

Appendix: Additional details and supporting documentation, including market research data, product specifications, client endorsements, and legal papers, were provided in the appendix.

Through the use of Harvard frameworks and methods, John produced a solid and thorough business plan. His careful examination of the market, straightforward value offer, and calculated planning set GreenTech Solutions up for success.

John's business plan served as a strategic roadmap for the expansion and advancement of the firm and was more than simply a piece of paper.

It aided him in obtaining capital, drawing in elite personnel, and forming alliances with significant interests. Investors were confident in his vision and capacity to carry it out because of the plan's depth and clarity.

Final Thoughts

Creating a strong business strategy is an essential first step for every firm. It offers a road map for achievement, directing your strategic choices and assisting you in overcoming the difficulties of becoming an entrepreneur. You may write a thorough and successful business plan that puts your company on the right track by knowing the fundamental elements of one and using strategic frameworks.

The success of a well-written company strategy is shown by the tales of Alex and John. They succeeded in identifying possibilities, setting themselves apart from competitors, and achieving their corporate objectives thanks to their careful study, strategic thinking, and meticulous preparation. Their stories serve as a reminder of how crucial clarity, readiness, and flexibility are to the entrepreneurial process.

These are some inspiring tales to consider before you set out on your own entrepreneurial adventure. Take the time and put in the work to draft a solid business plan that outlines your objectives, strategy, and vision. Make use of the frameworks and resources at your disposal, and be ready to modify and adapt as you gain knowledge and experience.

This is the realm of strategic planning; welcome. You may create a company that has a significant impact and realize your entrepreneurial aspirations with the help of a strong business plan.

CHAPTER 4

GETTING FUNDS FOR YOUR STARTUP

Comprehending Various Funding Choices

A startup's fundraising journey is a crucial part of its narrative. It is the resource that turns ideas into reality and the gasoline that propels your aspirations. It might be intimidating to navigate the financial choice landscape, but it's important to know what possibilities are available. Let's go on this adventure with Sarah, a recent graduate of Harvard Business School who looked into a number of financing sources before launching her health tech company, Healthify.

Bootstrapping: Sarah started out on her adventure using this method. She created the first version of the smartphone app Healthify, which aims to make managing chronic illness easier for patients, using money she saved up for herself. She was able to maintain complete control over her business by bootstrapping, making quick choices, and ensuring the result reflected her vision. However, as the expenses of development, marketing, and scaling increased, it became quickly clear that personal money could not support this.

Friends and Family: Sarah looked to her close friends and family as her money began to run low. She contacted her loved ones, sharing her idea and asking for their help. Despite being less formal and often more flexible, this financing method has its own set of drawbacks. Sarah had to strike a balance between the demands of her company as a professional and the emotional complexities of her personal connections.

Luckily, her close friends and family supported her vision and gave her the much-needed start-up money she needed to finish the project and start a pilot program.

Angel Investors: Sarah wanted to grow Healthify after a successful pilot and encouraging comments from early consumers. She made contact with angel investors, who are affluent people who would fund early-stage companies in return for shares. These investors often provide insightful networking opportunities, guidance, and expertise. Sarah put up a strong proposal that highlighted the distinct value proposition, market potential, and early traction of her solution. She was able to get finance and strategic counsel from an angel investor with experience in the healthcare industry.

Venture Capital: Sarah knew she needed a

significant amount of funding to support Healthify's quick development and enlarge her staff as the company started to take off. She went to venture capital (VC) companies, which make large investments in return for stock and often participate actively in the strategic direction of the business. Obtaining venture capital investment was a difficult and competitive procedure. Sarah honed her company plan, went to a lot of pitch sessions, and presented thorough financial estimates. Her perseverance paid off when she was able to get a Series A investment from a respectable venture capital company, which allowed Healthify to grow its business, improve its technology, and enter new markets.

Crowdfunding: In an effort to interact with prospective customers and test new features, Sarah also looked into crowdfunding during a product growth phase. Sites such as Kickstarter and Indiegogo provided a means of raising money and cultivating a fan base at the same time. Sarah started a crowdsourcing campaign with well-defined objectives, interesting material, and alluring prizes for supporters. Along with extra funding, the campaign produced insightful market validation and early user feedback.

Government subsidies and contests: In addition, Sarah made use of non-dilutive financing sources, including startup contests and government subsidies. These choices offered financing without requiring ownership. She engaged in startup contests, carefully applying for funds targeted at health tech innovation and promoting Healthify's potential influence on healthcare. In addition to bringing in more money, winning a sizable grant and a startup competition raised Healthify's profile and reputation in the sector.

Attracting Capitalists: HBS Perspectives

Drawing in investors is a combination of art and science. There are a number of ideas and tactics that you can learn from Harvard Business School to greatly improve your chances of getting financing. Sarah used the following important lessons along her journey:

Write a Story That Sells: Investors are purchasing not just your goods but also your vision and narrative. With a focus on her own experiences that motivated her to address the healthcare issues encountered by individuals with chronic diseases, Sarah developed a gripping story around Healthify. She emphasized how her idea would really benefit people, which made it seem urgent and relevant.

Know Your Market: Prospective investors look for proof that you are well-versed in your industry. Sarah carried out in-depth market research, determining important trends, rivals, and the possible size of the market. She gave a convincing presentation of the facts, showcasing both her expertise and the significant potential that Healthify was trying to seize.

Show Traction: Results speak louder than words. Sarah displayed the early enrollment rates, user reviews, and effectiveness of Healthify's pilot program. She presented data that showed user engagement, growth, and successful results, making a compelling argument for the potential of her company.

Create a Powerful Team: People are just as important to investors as ideas. Sarah emphasized the knowledge, abilities, and dedication of her team to Healthify's purpose. She highlighted how her team's combined background in technology, business management, and healthcare made them well equipped to carry out the plan.

Be Open and Ready: Being ready and transparent fosters trust. Sarah made sure she had a clear company strategy, comprehensive financial predictions, and backup plans. She had well-thought-out plans to deal with any dangers or difficulties and was upfront about them. She gave her investors confidence with this degree of preparedness.

Leverage Networks: The HBS network's power is immeasurable. Sarah made use of her relationships with classmates, instructors, and graduates to get introductions to possible investors. These friendly greetings often resulted in more accommodating and productive meetings. She also looked to seasoned graduates who had successfully negotiated the financial environment for guidance and assistance.

Case Study: [Founder 3] and Their Funding Journey

Let's examine the financing process of David, a second HBS alumnus who started EcoInnovate, a business that creates environmentally friendly packaging.

Starting from scratch: David's quest started with a love of sustainability and a goal to cut down on plastic waste. Using his money, he founded EcoInnovate and created a cutting-edge biodegradable packaging material. Prototyping, proving viability, and a great deal of research and development were all part of the first phase.

David was able to improve his product via bootstrapping, but it also constrained his resources and slowed down development.

Friends and Family: David contacted friends and family after realizing he needed more money. With great enthusiasm, he presented his idea, highlighting the potential market for his solution and its influence on the environment. His immediate circle supported him in his endeavors and gave him the first funding required to complete the prototype and start small-scale manufacturing.

Angel Investors: David looked for angel funding after receiving encouraging feedback from early customers and having a functioning prototype. He used his contacts at HBS to meet possible investors, pitched at startup showcases, and went to networking events. When he was able to get money from an angel investor who appreciated his dedication to sustainability, his perseverance paid off. David was able to start market testing, refine the product, and increase manufacturing thanks to this investment.

Venture Capital: David planned for quick expansion and deeper market penetration as EcoInnovate started to gather momentum. He went to venture capital and focused on companies that used green technologies and sustainability. It was a difficult procedure that needed a lot of planning and pitch sessions. After much work, David was able to convince a venture capital company that EcoInnovate had the capacity to upend the packaging sector and provide Series A money. He was able to grow into new areas, recruit essential staff, and scale operations thanks to this significant investment.

Crowdfunding: David started a crowdfunding effort in order to verify new product lines and connect with more ecologically concerned customers. He produced interesting material, explained the advantages of his environmentally friendly packaging, and provided alluring incentives. Along with raising more money, the campaign created a network of people who supported EcoInnovate's goals.

Government Grants and Contests: David looked at non-dilutive financing options as well. He participated in startup contests and submitted applications for government funds aimed at environmental innovation. EcoInnovate's reputation and exposure were enhanced, and substantial funds were delivered without diluting equity via the win of a prestigious grant and a major competition.

David's financing path was characterized by calculated choices, tenacity, and a distinct goal.

He made use of a variety of financing sources, each appropriate for a distinct stage of his startup's development. David was able to establish a strong financial base for EcoInnovate by combining bootstrapping, friends and family, angel investment, venture capital, crowdsourcing, and non-dilutive finance.

Final Thoughts

Getting funding for your business is a complex process that calls for perseverance, adaptation, and strategic preparation. Knowing the many financing choices accessible will help you determine the best course for your firm at different phases of development, including angel investors, venture capital, crowdsourcing, bootstrapping, and non-dilutive investment.

Using the knowledge and tactics from Harvard Business School can greatly improve your capacity to draw in investors. A good financing plan must include telling a compelling narrative, proving market knowledge and traction, assembling a solid team, being open and organized, and using networks.

The many routes to obtaining funds are shown by the tales of Sarah and David. Their examples demonstrate the value of tenacity, foresight, and making the most of the resources at hand. You may successfully navigate the financial environment and get the funds required to realize your entrepreneurial goal by comprehending and putting these ideas to use.

When you go out on your financing adventure, keep in mind that it's not only about collecting money; it's also about developing connections, getting feedback on your idea, and setting up the necessary funds to support the expansion and success of your firm. Greetings from the world

of startup finance, where each step you take will get you one step closer to achieving your goals and leaving a lasting impression.

CHAPTER 5

PUTTING TOGETHER YOUR IDEAL GROUP

Team Dynamics' Significance

Putting together an ideal team in the startup sector is like laying the groundwork for a skyscraper. How strong, cohesive, and resilient your team is will determine how high and steady your business can go. Claire's story, about a Harvard Business School alumna who started PayBright, a cutting-edge finance firm, eloquently highlights the vital significance of team relationships.

Creating a Vision Together: Claire's goal for PayBright was to transform the financial management of small companies by providing everyone access to cutting-edge financial tools. But she also understood that more than her experience and enthusiasm would be needed to make her idea a reality. It required teamwork, with each team member contributing special talents and sharing the same fundamental principles. Claire made sure that every prospective team member understood PayBright's purpose and principles by outlining them in detail beforehand.

Complementary talents and roles: Having the smartest people on the team isn't enough to create a dream team; they also need to make sure that their talents complement one another. A diverse range of skills were required by Claire, including programmers to develop the platform, financial specialists to guarantee legal compliance, marketers to disseminate the word, and customer service representatives to keep users. She painstakingly determined which positions were essential to PayBright's success and looked for people whose abilities addressed those particular needs. Claire, for example, teamed up with her classmate Mark, a software wizard with an eye for financial solutions, and Sarah, a marketing pro with a history of successful campaigns.

Cultural Fit and Adaptability: The importance of cultural fit extends beyond education and experience. Claire thought that a group with similar work ethics and ideals would function well together. She concentrated on hiring individuals that shared PayBright's values of creativity, honesty, and customer-focusedness in addition to being competent. She also emphasized flexibility, realizing that those who could flourish in a fast-paced startup environment were necessary given the ongoing difficulties and change.

Collaboration and Communication: The foundation of every successful team is effective cooperation and communication. Open conversation and free exchange of ideas were encouraged in Claire's surroundings. PayBright's operations relied heavily on brainstorming sessions, regular team meetings, and open decision-making procedures. Because of Claire's democratic and inclusive leadership style, every team member was made to feel important and heard.

Harvard Employment Practices

Harvard Business School emphasizes the value of strategic recruiting and team building while providing its students with cutting-edge recruitment tactics and procedures. Claire used a number of these strategies to assemble her ideal

PayBright team.

Behavioral Interviews: Using behavioral interviews was one of the most important skills Claire picked up at HBS. Using a candidate's prior conduct as a predictor of future performance is the main goal of this approach. Claire crafted interview questions that probed applicants' problem-solving skills, collaboration experiences, and alignment with PayBright's fundamental principles. She was able to assess applicants' interpersonal skills, cultural fit, and technical proficiency thanks to this method.

Case Studies and Practical Exams: Claire included case studies and practical exams in the hiring process to evaluate applicants' practical skills. She gave applicants real-world difficulties to solve while hiring technical staff members. She urged applicants to create campaigns based on hypothetical circumstances for marketing roles. Claire was able to assess applicants' inventiveness, problem-solving abilities, and capacity to apply information in real-world contexts thanks to this practical method.

Networking and Referrals: Harvard's vast alumni network and its networking-friendly culture are great tools for hiring. Claire made use of her contacts at HBS to ask for recommendations and referrals. She went to networking events, alumni reunions, and industry functions to meet possible employers and learn from mentors and colleagues. This approach gave her a better grasp of market trends and best practices, in addition to assisting her in identifying outstanding talent.

Internship Programs: Claire also used project-based employment and internships as a successful recruiting tactic. Using this method, she was able to watch prospective employees in action, rate their performance, and determine whether or not they would fit in with PayBright's principles and culture. Promising interns were often extended offers of full-time jobs, which facilitated a seamless transition and decreased the risks related to new hiring.

Diversity and Inclusion: Claire discovered at HBS how crucial these elements are to creating a strong, creative team. She made a conscious effort to assemble a diverse staff because she knew that a range of viewpoints and experiences encourage innovation and improve decision-making. Claire established fair hiring procedures, made sure everyone felt welcome, and promoted diversity as a key PayBright value.

Case Study: [Founder 4] and Their Achievements in Team Building

Let's examine the experience of Michael, an additional HBS alumnus who started GreenWave, a business dedicated to creating sustainable technology for urban settings, to further highlight the importance of putting together a dream team.

The Vision and Early Stages: Michael had big plans for GreenWave. He wanted to turn cities into efficient, sustainable ecosystems by developing clever, environmentally friendly solutions. But he was aware that realizing this goal would require assembling a group of specialists who were as passionate about sustainability and innovation as he was. Michael's path started at HBS with a small but committed group of like-minded people who each brought their own special talents and viewpoints to the table.

Strategic Recruitment: Michael needed to grow his staff as GreenWave started to take off. He used a number of Harvard strategies for tactical hiring. Recognizing the need for a solid foundation, he concentrated on employing people who shared GreenWave's beliefs and purpose in addition to having the requisite talents.

Michael evaluated applicants' prior experiences and approaches to sustainability issues via behavioral interviews. He included hands-on assessments to gauge their capacity for original thought and problem-solving. For example, applicants for engineering positions were requested to devise environmentally friendly solutions for typical urban issues, while candidates for business development positions were encouraged to establish plans for breaking into new markets.

Using Networks and Referrals: Michael made great use of his connections at HBS to find candidates. He asked for references and referrals from instructors, former students, and professionals in the field. Using this method, he was able to find outstanding talent that had previously been screened by reliable sources. In order to meet possible candidates and learn about new trends and technology, Michael also went to industry conferences and networking functions.

Creating an Inclusive and Diverse Team: Michael was dedicated to creating an inclusive and diverse team at GreenWave. He felt that the team's ability to solve problems would be improved and creativity would be stimulated by a diverse range of perspectives, backgrounds, and experiences. To create a fair and inclusive recruiting process, Michael adopted impartial recruitment techniques, including organized interviews and blind resume evaluations. Additionally, he established a welcoming workplace where each team member felt encouraged to share their thoughts and was appreciated.

Team Dynamics and Collaboration: Recognizing the value of team dynamics, Michael promoted an environment at GreenWave that values open communication and teamwork. He promoted brainstorming sessions, cross-functional initiatives, and frequent team meetings to make sure that everyone was on the same page and pursuing the same objectives. Because of Michael's inclusive and participative leadership style, team members were given the freedom to choose and the assistance they needed to be successful.

Success and Growth: His ideal team came together thanks to a calculated strategy. Investors, clients, and partners took notice of and expressed interest in GreenWave's creative solutions. Because of the team's varied skill set and spirit of cooperation, they were able to take on challenging projects and create innovative solutions that helped GreenWave stand out from the competition.

A noteworthy accomplishment was the creation of a smart water management system, which resulted in a 30% decrease in water use in cities. In order to build, execute, and optimize the system, engineers, data scientists, and urban planners collaborated on the project. This achievement demonstrated the team's technical skill as well as the value of cooperation and a common goal.

Michael was dedicated to building a solid team culture even as GreenWave expanded. He made investments in training for team members, offered chances for lifelong learning, and made sure the fundamental principles of sustainability, creativity, and inclusion were respected. The group's accomplishments served as a testimony to the value of putting together a dream team as well as the influence that smart hiring and team dynamics have on the expansion and success of startups.

Final Thoughts

Putting together your ideal team is a crucial step in creating a profitable firm. Effective team composition, tactical hiring procedures, and a robust inclusive and collaborative culture may make a big difference in your startup's capacity to develop, flourish, and innovate.

Michael's adventure with GreenWave and Claire's experience with PayBright serve as examples of the strength of a well-assembled team. Through an emphasis on complimentary abilities, cultural fit, efficient communication, and the use of Harvard recruiting practices, they successfully built robust and cohesive teams that propelled their firms to unprecedented heights.

Your team is your most valuable resource as you start your business adventure. Spend time and energy finding the ideal candidates, creating a welcoming and cooperative work atmosphere, and cultivating a culture of common goals and values. In the world of startups, you may realize your idea and succeed spectacularly if you have your dream team by your side. Greetings and welcome to the thrilling adventure of team-building, where each team member's input helps your project reach its final objectives.

CHAPTER 6

INNOVATION AND PRODUCT DEVELOPMENT

The Development Process: From Idea to Market

A concept is the foundation of every successful company, but developing an idea into a commercially viable product is a dynamic and intricate process. Let's follow Sam's path, a Harvard Business School alumnus who created EcoTech, a business dedicated to creating smart home energy solutions, to get an understanding of this journey.

Conceptualizing the Idea: Sam was personally frustrated by excessive energy costs and ineffective household energy systems, which served as the impetus for EcoTech. He had an idea for a smart gadget that could minimize environmental effects, save expenses, and optimize energy use in real-time. Although the original idea was straightforward, it took a great deal of study and development to turn it into a workable product.

Market Research and Feasibility Studies: Sam's product development process began with a comprehensive market research study. He examined current solutions, pinpointed client pain areas, and examined the energy industry. He was able to improve his idea and get important insights into the possible market for his product thanks to this study. In order to evaluate the idea's technical and financial viability, Sam also carried out feasibility studies. Cost analysis, resource needs, and the possible return on investment were all covered in these studies.

Prototype and Testing: Sam advanced to the prototype stage after gaining a thorough grasp of the market and viability. To produce the first iteration of EcoTech's smart gadget, he brought together a small group of engineers and designers. Iterative design, testing, and refining were all part of this phase. The group constructed many prototypes, fixing errors and adding enhancements in response to test results. Sam realized that thorough testing was necessary to guarantee the usability, dependability, and functioning of the product.

User Feedback and Iteration: Sam gathered input from users to improve the product after creating a functional prototype. To get feedback from possible clients, he ran focus groups, pilot projects, and beta testing. This input was very helpful in pointing out problems with usability, new features, and possible enhancements. Based on these comments, Sam's team made adjustments to the product design such that the finished version satisfied customer requirements and expectations.

Scaling Production: Sam had to deal with the difficulty of increasing production when the product was optimized. In order to manufacture the smart gadgets in large quantities without sacrificing their quality or affordability, he teamed up with a manufacturer. Contract negotiations, supply chain setup, and quality control implementation were all part of this phase. Sam also concentrated on streamlining manufacturing procedures to save expenses and boost effectiveness.

Launching the Product: Sam organized a calculated launch once the product was prepared for the market. In order to reach his target demographic, he created a thorough marketing and distribution plan that made use of both physical and internet platforms. The marketing campaign emphasized the distinct advantages of EcoTech's smart gadget, stressing its effectiveness, affordability, and environmental impact. Sam generated excitement and drove early sales via influencer collaborations, social media, and media attention.

Post-Launch Support and Improvement: After the product was launched, the development process continued. Sam was dedicated to client satisfaction and ongoing development. To resolve consumer concerns, get input, and provide updates, he set up a strong customer service infrastructure. Sam's group also worked on adding new features and improvements in response to market trends and customer input, making sure EcoTech's product was cutting-edge and competitive.

Innovation: Staying on the Cutting Edge

Innovation is essential to staying ahead of the curve in the fast-paced world of startups. Businesses that don't innovate run the danger of becoming out of style. Sam's experience with EcoTech serves as an example of how success and expansion may be fueled by ongoing innovation.

Building an Invention Culture: Sam realized that invention was an ongoing activity rather than a one-time event. He promoted an innovative culture at EcoTech by motivating his staff to think outside the box, question the status quo, and consider novel concepts. EcoTech's culture included frequent brainstorming meetings, innovation workshops, and a welcoming atmosphere where failure was seen as a teaching opportunity.

Investing in Research and Development: A key component of EcoTech's innovation strategy was consistent funding for research and development (R&D). Sam invested a lot of money in R&D to make sure his team had the equipment, know-how, and support they needed to continue leading the way in innovation. This was a wise investment since EcoTech continuously created new features, enhanced their current lineup, and looked into untapped markets.

Remaining Customer-Centric: EcoTech's innovation was propelled by a thorough comprehension of its clients' requirements and preferences. Sam's team regularly gathered input and ideas from clients in order to guide their efforts toward innovation. They tracked consumer behavior, saw patterns, and projected demands using data analytics. Because of this focus on the needs of the consumer, EcoTech's inventions were useful and relevant to its customers.

Using Technology and Trends: Sam and his group closely monitored new developments in the industry as well as developments in technology. They were early users of cutting-edge technology, including the Internet of Things (IoT), machine learning, and artificial intelligence (AI), in their products to improve usability and functionality. EcoTech stayed one step ahead of the competition in the industry by keeping on top of technical developments.

Networking and Collaboration: Collaboration is a key factor in the success of innovation. Sam formed alliances with other companies, academic institutions, and business leaders by using his HBS network. These partnerships made new concepts, tools, and resources available. For instance, EcoTech was able to carry out cutting-edge research on energy optimization algorithms thanks to a collaboration with a prestigious institution, which resulted in notable product advancements.

Case Study: [Founder 5] and Their Innovative Approach

To demonstrate the efficacy of innovation in product creation, let us examine the experiences of Emma, a fellow HBS alumna who established GreenPulse, an enterprise specializing in sustainable energy solutions.

Identifying a Unique Opportunity: Emma was motivated to start GreenPulse by the increasing need for clean energy on a worldwide scale as well as the difficulties in incorporating renewable energy sources into the current electrical systems. She saw a rare chance to create a clever energy management system that would improve grid stability and maximize the use of renewable energy sources.

Innovative Product Concept: Emma combined smart grid management software with cutting-edge energy storage technology in a novel way. The idea was to develop a system that could effectively distribute energy, store surplus renewable energy, and provide grid operators with real-time information. This would increase grid dependability, minimize the usage of fossil fuels, and boost the use of renewable energy.

Collaborative Development: Emma started off by putting together a multidisciplinary group of professionals with backgrounds in data analytics, software development, and energy technology. She also collaborated with leaders in business and academia to make use of their resources and experience. This cooperative approach meant that GreenPulse's solution was founded on a solid foundation of innovation and expertise while also speeding up the development process.

Prototyping and Pilot Projects: Developing many prototypes and putting them to the test in actual situations were part of GreenPulse's product development process. Emma conducted trial initiatives in conjunction with utility providers to collect information and understand the functionality of the system. These pilot programs were essential for improving the product, seeing possible problems, and persuading stakeholders of its worth.

Securing financing for innovation: Emma was aware that significant financing was needed for ongoing innovation. She was able to get government funding and venture finance for renewable energy innovation by using her contacts at HBS. Thanks to this financing, GreenPulse was able to grow its operations, increase its R&D activities, and invest in cutting-edge technology.

Market introduction and adoption: Utility companies, legislators, and environmental organizations greeted GreenPulse's smart energy management system introduction with excitement. Emma's well-thought-out marketing strategy emphasized how the technology might boost grid efficiency, lower carbon emissions, and better integrate renewable energy sources. Following a successful debut, GreenPulse gained considerable traction and established itself as a pioneer in the renewable energy industry.

Ongoing Enhancement and Growth: GreenPulse's innovation didn't end with the debut of its first product. Emma's team persisted in getting input, examining performance information, and creating new features. To further increase their market reach, they added solutions for both residential and business consumers to their product portfolio. Emma's dedication to ongoing enhancement meant that GreenPulse was always at the forefront of innovation in renewable energy.

Impact and Recognition: The renewable energy sector was greatly impacted by GreenPulse's novel strategy. Because of the system's capacity to maximize energy distribution and storage, more renewable energy sources are being used, which lowers greenhouse gas emissions and advances sustainability. Emma and her colleagues further solidified GreenPulse's reputation and impact by winning many accolades and recognition for their efforts to innovate clean energy.

Final Thoughts

Innovation and product development are essential to every successful business. From concept to market, the process requires careful planning, extensive testing, and ongoing improvement. Sam's experience with EcoTech and Emma's journey with GreenPulse serve as examples of the value of an organized development process, an innovative culture, and a customer-focused methodology.

Innovation is a continuous dedication to quality and advancement rather than a one-time occurrence. Startups may maintain their lead and achieve long-term success by cultivating a culture of innovation, investing in research and development, paying attention to consumer demands, using new technology, and working together with partners.

Remember these tales as you set out on your own product development journey. Accept the chances and risks that come with innovation, but don't waver from your goal. You can transform your ideas into products that are marketable and have a significant effect if you have the correct team, mentality, and strategy. Greetings from the fascinating realm of invention and product creation, where each step you take will get you one step closer to realizing your dream.

CHAPTER 7

MARKETING AND BRANDING

Developing an Engaging Brand Narrative

Effective branding and marketing start with a strong brand narrative. It takes more than simply product placement to engage your audience on an emotional level. Let's follow the path of Lily, a Harvard Business School graduate who launched the eco-friendly skincare business PureNature, to demonstrate the potency of a well-crafted brand narrative.

Uncovering the Story: Lily's love of natural skincare and her worries about the dangerous ingredients in traditional beauty products served as the impetus for PureNature. Her goal was to establish a brand that focused on sustainability, purity, and the therapeutic value of nature. She was aware, however, that in order to stand out in the congested skin care industry, she would need a brand narrative that would captivate customers and really connect with them.

Building a Relationship with the Audience: Lily began by determining who her target market was: people who were worried about environmental sustainability and health and cared about what they put on their skin. To comprehend their wants, attitudes, and preferences, she carried out a thorough analysis of market research. According to her audience's study, they were interested in skincare products that worked, but they also wanted to support companies that shared their values and supported social causes.

Creating the Story: Lily used these observations to create the brand narrative for

PureNature. She spoke about her own experience dealing with skin problems and learning about the therapeutic properties of natural substances. She discussed how her grandmother's traditional herbal treatments served as inspiration for the creation of a skincare brand that respected the knowledge of nature. The brand narrative highlighted PureNature's dedication to sustainability, purity, and ethical ingredient sourcing.

Visual and Verbal Identity: The visual representation of a brand narrative is just as important as the words used to tell it. Lily collaborated with a branding firm to develop a visual style that embodied the principles of Pure Nature. Earthy hues, a simple style, and pictures of natural components were all used in the package design. The brand's emblem, a tiny leaf, stood for purity, development, and a link to the natural world. The tone of the brand was peaceful, caring, and educational, reflecting the experience of using PureNature goods.

Introducing the Audience: Lily shared the PureNature brand narrative on many channels. She started a blog where she discussed the value of sustainability, the advantages of natural skincare products, and the backstories of each component. She engaged the public via social media by sharing consumer testimonials, eco-friendly practices, and behind-the-scenes looks at product development. Lily further engaged in partnerships with beauty bloggers and influencers that shared PureNature's principles in order to enhance the brand's narrative.

Harvard Methods for Successful Marketing

Students at Harvard Business School are prepared with cutting-edge marketing techniques that prioritize creative thinking, customer-centricity, and data-driven decision-making. Lily used a number of Harvard strategies to design and carry out a successful PureNature marketing campaign.

Market Segmentation and Targeting: The significance of market segmentation and targeting was one of the fundamental strategies Lily discovered at HBS. She could focus her marketing efforts on certain groups by breaking the larger market into smaller, more manageable divisions. Lily divided her audience into groups according to age, lifestyle, skincare issues, and environmental consciousness. She was able to produce tailored marketing messages as a result, appealing to each target demographic.

Value Proposition and Differentiation: Lily concentrated on precisely outlining PureNature's value proposition in order to make a name for herself in the cutthroat skincare industry. She emphasized the special qualities of her goods—all-natural, pure components, environmentally friendly packaging, and a dedication to sustainability. Additionally, she set PureNature apart from rivals by highlighting the company's ethical and transparent business methods. Customers who shared the brand's beliefs were drawn to PureNature thanks to its compelling value offer.

Integrated Marketing Communications: A consistent and coherent message must be used in all marketing channels in order for it to be effective. To guarantee that PureNature's brand narrative was conveyed consistently across all touchpoints—website, social media, email marketing, and retail locations—Lily put in place an integrated marketing communications (IMC) approach. With each consumer encounter, this strategy reaffirmed the brand's message and produced a cohesive brand experience.

Content Marketing and Storytelling: A key component of PureNature's marketing plan was content marketing. Lily used narrative techniques to provide interesting and educational material that taught her audience about sustainability and natural skincare. Video material, social media updates, and blog pieces were all created with the intention of educating the public and discreetly highlighting PureNature's offerings. This strategy promoted consumer loyalty and trust.

The Harvard Business School highlights the significance of using data to guide marketing tactics in its course on "Data-Driven Decision Making. Lily used powerful analytics software to monitor the effectiveness of her marketing initiatives. She kept an eye on indicators including customer reviews, social media engagement, website traffic, and conversion rates. She was able to determine what was effective, maximize her campaigns, and make wise choices thanks to her data-driven strategy.

Case Study: [Founder 6] and Their Branding Success

To demonstrate the power of strong branding and marketing, let's look at the story of Jake, a fellow HBS alumnus who started the cutting-edge electric bike startup GlowRide.

Identifying the Opportunity: Jake's passion for riding and his annoyance with urban pollutants and traffic jams served as the basis for GlowRide. He had an idea for a brand that supported healthy living and sustainable urban transportation. But as the electric bike business became more competitive, Jake realized that GlowRide needed to succeed in order to have a compelling brand narrative and powerful marketing.

Creating GlowRide's Brand Story: Jake began by outlining the three main principles of GlowRide: community, sustainability, and innovation. He created a brand narrative that highlighted the fun of riding, the advantages of electric bikes for city transportation, and the company's dedication to lowering carbon emissions. He spoke about how riding a bike in his city gave him a sense of freedom and enjoyment, and how this experience motivated him to develop a product that may revolutionize urban transportation.

Creating a Vibrant Visual Identity: Jake collaborated with a design group to develop a visual brand that embodied GlowRide's principles and drew in city travelers. The dynamic lightning bolt emblem in the brand's sleek, contemporary logo stood for energy, speed, and inventiveness. Vibrant blues and greens were used in the color scheme to represent sustainability and a novel approach to urban transportation. Every marketing piece, including product packaging, advertising materials, and the website, adhered to the same visual identity.

Using Harvard Marketing Tactics: Jake used a number of Harvard marketing tactics to develop a successful GlowRide marketing plan.

Market Research and Customer Insights: To better understand his target market, which consists of students, urban professionals, and eco-conscious commuters, Jake undertook a thorough study of the market. He discovered their wants, preferences, and sore spots using focus groups, polls, and social media analytics. GlowRide's price policy, marketing messaging, and product features were all influenced by this study.

Segmented Marketing Campaigns: Jake divided his audience into many categories, such as regular commuters, weekend riders, and fitness aficionados, based on his study. He developed marketing strategies that were specifically tailored to each market niche, emphasizing the features of GlowRide bikes that appealed to them. Campaigns targeting everyday commuters, for instance, emphasized savings and ease, but those aimed at exercise aficionados highlighted performance attributes and health advantages.

Influencer and Content Marketing Partnerships: Jake established a strong online presence for GlowRide via content marketing. He produced informative blog entries, films, and social media postings on electric bikes, sustainable transportation advice, and urban biking. In addition, he collaborated with cyclists and influencers who agreed with GlowRide's principles. These collaborations aided in expanding the brand's narrative and audience.

Experiential Marketing and Community Engagement: Jake used experiential marketing techniques to establish a stronger rapport with his target audience. He planned community gatherings where people could get a hands-on look at GlowRide bikes, including group rides, bike maintenance classes, and sustainability fairs. These gatherings promoted word-of-mouth advertising and helped create a sense of community around the brand.

Data-Driven Optimization: Jake collected client feedback and tracked the effectiveness of his marketing strategies using data analytics. He kept an eye on important data, including website traffic, social media interaction, sales conversions, and client happiness. He was able to see patterns, make wise judgments, and constantly refine his marketing campaigns thanks to this data-driven strategy.

Market Impact and Branding Success: GlowRide's successful marketing tactics and compelling brand narrative paid dividends. The business soon attracted a devoted clientele and rose to prominence among city commuters. Customers were moved by the brand's dedication to sustainability and innovation, and GlowRide bicycles came to represent environmentally responsible urban transportation.

A noteworthy accomplishment was GlowRide's collaboration with many large cities to introduce bike-sharing initiatives. This program increased revenue as well as the brand's reputation and exposure. Due to its creative strategy and powerful branding, GlowRide gained media attention, which resulted in articles in prestigious magazines and a rise in brand recognition.

Jake established GlowRide as a thought leader in the electric bike sector with his clever marketing initiatives. The company's social media pages and blog became the go-to places to get information on sustainable transportation and urban mobility. The reputation and impact of the brand were further enhanced by this thought leadership.

Final Thoughts

Branding and marketing are essential to a startup's success. A company's capacity to draw in and keep consumers may be greatly impacted by developing a strong visual identity, using data-driven marketing techniques, and creating an engaging brand narrative.

Jake's experience with GlowRide and Lily's trip with PureNature both demonstrate how crucial it is to distinguish your brand, know your target, and provide a unified and interesting brand experience. Through the use of Harvard's cutting-edge marketing strategies and a steadfast dedication to their core principles, both founders succeeded in building powerful brands.

Your brand story is more than simply a tale; it's

the core of your company's identity and the secret to engaging your audience as you set out on your own marketing and branding journey. Adopt a narrative approach, using data to guide your tactics, and adhere to your brand's core principles. With the appropriate strategy, you can develop a brand that connects with consumers, propels the expansion of your firm, and accomplishment. Greetings from the fascinating realm of branding and marketing, where each choice you make moves you one step closer to creating a name that people remember.

CHAPTER 8

EXPANDING YOUR COMPANY

Techniques for Long-Term Development

For any startup, scaling a firm is an exciting and difficult stage. It necessitates resource allocation, strategic planning, and the capacity for situational flexibility. Let's examine the story of FitPro, a fitness technology firm created by Alex, a Harvard Business School alumnus, in order to get an understanding of the complexities of growing.

Building the Foundation: When Alex first started FitPro, the company's main goal was to create fitness software that integrated dietary advice with individualized exercise regimens. Although the app initially garnered popularity,

Alex realized he needed a clear and scalable business plan in order to achieve sustained development. He began by outlining FitPro's key advantages, which include cutting-edge technology, a sizable user base, and a dedication to client happiness.

Creating a Scalable Infrastructure: Making sure FitPro's infrastructure could support rising demand was the first step in growing the business. Alex made a significant investment in reliable cloud-based technology to handle an increasing user base and guarantee flawless app operation. Additionally, he concentrated on automating crucial procedures, including data analytics, assistance, and client onboarding. The organization was able to accommodate a higher number of consumers without sacrificing quality because of this automation.

Expanding the Product Line: Alex made the

decision to broaden FitPro's product offering in order to draw in more customers and generate more income. He unveiled new features, including live coaching sessions, virtual fitness courses, and wearable device integration. Along with improving the app's value proposition, these changes made it possible to reach new markets and clientele. In order to generate a consistent flow of recurring income, Alex also created a subscription model that offered premium content and services for a monthly charge.

Market Penetration and Expansion: Entering new markets is a common step in growing a firm. Alex carried out an in-depth market analysis to determine possible FitPro growth areas. He examined elements like the competitive landscape, market size, and regulatory framework. He focused on overseas countries with strong smartphone penetration and rising interest in fitness based on his results. Through careful consideration of the language and cultural quirks of these new markets, Alex modified his marketing techniques to ensure a seamless launch and favorable response.

Hiring and Team Building: As FitPro expanded, Alex came to understand how crucial it was to assemble a solid team to help with the business's growth. He concentrated on employing people who not only brought a variety of talents and knowledge to the table but also shared his vision and beliefs. In order to find top talent, Alex established a strict hiring procedure and made investments in employee development plans. He made sure his staff was inspired and equipped to propel FitPro's expansion by cultivating a creative and cooperative work atmosphere.

Maintaining client focus: Alex was dedicated to keeping a laser-like focus on client satisfaction even as FitPro grew. He put in place procedures for collecting and evaluating consumer input, utilizing it to guide future developments and enhancements to the product. In addition, Alex placed a high priority on providing exceptional customer service, making sure that consumers got prompt assistance. Long-term success requires loyalty and trust, both of which were fostered by this customer-centric strategy.

Overcoming Difficulties in Scaling

Growing a firm has its own unique set of difficulties. From overcoming operational challenges to upholding corporate culture, it calls for strategic planning and flexibility.

Throughout his ascent through FitPro, Alex encountered a number of difficulties, but his proactive demeanor and aptitude for problem-solving enabled him to get over them.

Managing Operational Complexity: FitPro faced considerable challenges in managing the additional operational complexity that came with its expansion. Alex had to deal with problems with logistics, quality assurance, and supply chain management. In order to tackle this, he put in place strong operational procedures and made investments in technological solutions that provide real-time operational insights. In order to make sure that partners and suppliers could satisfy the rising demand while upholding strict quality requirements, Alex also worked closely with them.

Balancing Growth and Quality: Sometimes rapid expansion is accompanied by a drop in customer service or product quality. Alex was determined to stay clear of this hazard. He put in place stringent quality control procedures and kept a close eye on key performance indicators (KPIs) to make sure FitPro's products remained superior. Additionally, Alex established cross-functional teams that collaborated to maintain a high standard of service and quickly resolve any concerns.

Securing Funding for Growth: Growing a company often requires a substantial outlay of cash. Alex had to deal with the difficulty of finding money to support FitPro's growth objectives. Utilizing his Harvard connections, he made connections with possible investors and created thorough business plans and financial estimates. In addition, Alex took part in startup contests and pitch events, showcasing FitPro's accomplishments and future development. His perseverance paid off, as he was able to get financing from angels and venture capitalists in many rounds.

Maintaining Company Culture: FitPro faced growing challenges in maintaining its culture as it expanded. Alex recognized that employee engagement and retention depended on a strong corporate culture. He placed a strong emphasis on honest communication, openness, and a common goal. In addition, Alex planned frequent team-building exercises and promoted a positive work-life balance. He made sure FitPro's culture held true as the business grew by creating a welcoming and healthy work atmosphere.

Adjusting to Market Shifts: The fitness sector is dynamic, with shifting customer tastes and trends on a regular basis. Alex had to make sure FitPro stayed relevant while keeping ahead of market trends. He was quick to modify his plans in response to competition activity and industry changes, which he closely monitored. FitPro was able to remain competitive and inventive because of Alex's agility and vision, which she demonstrated by harnessing emerging technology and implementing new fitness trends into the app.

Case Study: [Founder 7] and Their Growth Journey

Let us explore the narrative of Mia, an additional HBS alumna who started the sustainable fashion firm EcoLuxe, in order to demonstrate the fundamentals of developing a business.

Spotting the Opportunity: Mia's interest in fashion and sustainability was the driving force behind her trip. She saw that there was a rising market for clothes made ethically and environmentally, but many of the firms didn't live up to the hype in terms of quality and appearance. Mia recognized a chance to launch a company that catered to customers who wanted to appear stylish but also make eco-friendly decisions by fusing high fashion with sustainability.

Creating a Scalable Business Model: Mia set out to create a scalable business plan for EcoLuxe right away. She found eco-friendly materials and collaborated with moral producers, who could expand output as demand grew. In order to preserve greater profit margins, collect useful data, and manage the client experience, Mia also adopted a direct-to-consumer (DTC) business strategy.

Creating Brand Awareness: Mia was aware that expanding EcoLuxe would require creating brand awareness. To reach her target audience, she made use of influencer marketing and social media. Through partnerships with environmental activists and fashion influencers, Mia promoted EcoLuxe's message and highlighted its distinctive selling point. Her deft use of visually attractive and captivating content created buzz for the brand and helped cultivate a devoted following.

Expanding Product Offerings: Mia increased the range of products offered by EcoLuxe in order to maintain growth. In order to accommodate a variety of client tastes and events, she debuted new collections that included seasonal lines and accessories. Customers were more loyal as a result of the diversification of income sources and the increasing availability of eco-friendly items under the EcoLuxe brand.

Improving Customer Experience: Mia

concentrated on giving customers a smooth and enjoyable experience. She made investments in a website that is easy to use, expedited the buying process, and put customized marketing plans into action. Mia placed a high value on providing exceptional customer service, making sure that questions and problems were resolved right away. She generated recurring business and cultivated strong connections with her clients by improving the whole customer experience.

International Expansion: After making a name for herself in the home market, Mia turned her attention to growth abroad. She carried out market research to identify areas where interest in sustainable fashion is rising, and she created entrance tactics specifically for each of those areas. Mia worked with regional influencers and merchants to increase brand recognition and customized EcoLuxe's marketing messaging to appeal to local consumers. Her calculated approach to global growth enabled EcoLuxe to establish a presence in important areas and increase its worldwide footprint.

Navigating Growing Challenges: EcoLuxe encountered a number of difficulties, much like every growing company. Mia had to deal with problems with the supply chain, handle more complicated operations, and preserve product quality. She overcomes these obstacles by establishing trusting relationships with suppliers, making technological investments, and putting strict quality control procedures in place. Mia's ability to solve problems and take initiative helped EcoLuxe overcome these obstacles and maintain its development trajectory.

Achieving Sustainable Growth: Mia's calculated approach to growing and EcoLuxe's dedication to sustainability paid dividends. The company expanded significantly and attracted a devoted and varied clientele. Customers were drawn to EcoLuxe's creative designs and moral business methods, which helped the company stand out in the cutthroat fashion sector. EcoLuxe's quick and sustainable expansion was made possible by Mia's ability to adjust to shifting market circumstances while keeping a laser-like focus on sustainability.

Final Thoughts

The process of scaling a firm is intricate and multidimensional, requiring thoughtful preparation, astute judgment, and flexibility in response to changing conditions. The experiences of Alex with FitPro and Mia with EcoLuxe serve as reminders of how crucial it is to develop a scalable infrastructure, increase the range of products offered, improve customer service, and manage the difficulties that occur with business expansion.

Maintaining product quality, operational effectiveness, and corporate culture are all important components of sustainable growth strategies, in addition to boosting revenue and market share. Both Alex and Mia were successful in scaling their firms and achieving long-term development by using the cutting-edge strategies and insights offered by Harvard Management School.

As you go out on your own scaling path, keep in mind that expansion needs to be planned and deliberate. Prioritize establishing a solid foundation, comprehending your target market, and making ongoing improvements to your goods and services. You may overcome scaling obstacles and achieve sustained company development with the appropriate strategy.

Greetings from the fascinating realm of scaling, where each step you take will get your firm closer to reaching its full potential.

CHAPTER 9

OVERCOMING OBSTACLES AND SETBACKS

Typical Startup Errors and Solutions

Establishing a company is a difficult path fraught with dangers. Numerous business owners encounter obstacles that, if not appropriately handled, might impede their advancement. Let's examine the background of Emily, a Harvard Business School alumna who started TechGenius, an edtech company that offers students individualized learning experiences, in order to have a better understanding of these difficulties.

Lack of Market Research: Ignoring comprehensive market research is one of the most frequent mistakes made by entrepreneurs. Emily thought that her novel approach to individualized learning would draw a sizable clientele when she founded TechGenius. She soon discovered, however, that she hadn't completely grasped the requirements and preferences of her intended audience. The first adoption was sluggish, and Emily had trouble getting momentum.

Avoiding the Pitfall: Emily did extensive market research to change her direction. To learn about the expectations and pain areas of instructors, parents, and prospective users, she solicited input. She was able to better satisfy the demands of her audience by customizing TechGenius's services with the aid of this study.

Emily made sure her product connected with the target market by giving market research first priority, which eventually increased user engagement.

Inadequate Financial Planning: Inadequate financial planning is a significant additional risk. Emily first misjudged the expenses associated with creating and promoting TechGenius. She was in danger of having to suspend operations due to a cash flow issue. Emily found it difficult to keep track of her spending and get more money in the absence of a defined financial strategy.

Avoiding the Pitfall: Emily asked mentors and financial specialists in her Harvard network for help. She created a thorough financial strategy that included cash flow management, forecasting, and budgeting. Emily was able to stabilize TechGenius's financial status and attract investors who were impressed by her rigorous approach by regularly monitoring her finances and making necessary adjustments to her tactics.

expanding Too Quickly: Growing slowly might be just as risky as expanding too quickly. Emily was eager to grow and tried to scale TechGenius too soon, which resulted in a drop in product quality and operational inefficiencies. As a result of the company's limited resources, consumer satisfaction started to decline.

Avoiding the Pitfall: After realizing her error, Emily took her time climbing. She concentrated on making sure that TechGenius's key competencies were strengthened and that the product maintained its high caliber. Emily also made investments in her team's education and training, preparing them to manage expansion more skillfully. She maintained growth without sacrificing quality by taking a deliberate approach to growing.

Disregarding input: Believing they know what's best for their firm, some entrepreneurs make the mistake of disregarding input. Emily first discounted criticism about TechGenius's user interface, believing it to be a little problem. But as consumer annoyance increased, churns and bad reviews followed.

Stepping Ahead: Emily discovered the value of paying attention to her clients. She put in place a strong feedback system that lets people provide recommendations and experiences. Through proactive responses to comments and ongoing enhancements, Emily improved TechGenius's reputation while also improving the user experience.

Failure-Related Lessons: HBS Views

Students at Harvard Business School are taught that failure is not fatal but rather a priceless teaching tool. If failure is seen with the correct attitude, it may provide insights that pave the way for future success. Let's examine how Emily was able to use her obstacles as learning opportunities thanks to HBS's thoughts on failure.

Embracing a Growth Mentality: HBS emphasizes the value of a growth mentality, pushing students to see setbacks as chances for personal development rather than as obstacles to overcome. Emily took on this attitude, seeing every obstacle as an opportunity to grow. This viewpoint enabled her to maintain her fortitude and drive in the face of adversity.

Analyzing Failures Objectively: Relying on non-emotional judgment to examine failures objectively is a crucial takeaway from HBS. After TechGenius encountered problems, Emily carried out in-depth post-mortems to determine the underlying causes and draw lessons from them. She was able to make wise selections and steer clear of making the same errors thanks to her analytical approach.

Seeking Mentorship and Support: HBS places a strong emphasis on the benefits of peer support and mentoring. Emily made use of her HBS network to get guidance from mentors and seasoned business owners. Their advice on strategic choices as well as their support and insights enabled her to overcome obstacles with greater effectiveness.

Iterative Improvement: HBS emphasizes the value of gradual, small-scale modifications as opposed to radical overhauls. Emily used TechGenius to develop incremental adjustments based on performance metrics and customer input. She was able to develop a more reliable product and advance steadily thanks to her strategy.

Adaptability and Perseverance: Two essential qualities for entrepreneurs are flexibility and perseverance. HBS encourages students to maintain a flexible approach while remaining true to their goal. Emily's flexibility enabled her to change course and modify her approach as necessary, while her tenacity kept her focused on TechGenius's goal.

Case Study: [Founder 8] and Their Turnaround Story

In order to demonstrate how overcoming obstacles and setbacks may result in achievement, allow us to explore the tale of Ryan, an additional HBS alumni who established GreenWave, an eco-friendly seafood enterprise.

The First Battle: Ryan's goal for GreenWave was to use cutting-edge aquaculture technology and sustainable methods to completely transform the seafood business. On the other hand, the first stage proved difficult. The business encountered operational inefficiencies, regulatory obstacles, and opposition from conventional fish suppliers. Ryan was passionate and committed, but GreenWave was unable to establish itself in the market.

Facing Financial Crisis: When GreenWave encountered a serious financial crisis, it was one of the most difficult obstacles to overcome. The business made significant infrastructural investments and overestimated the demand for its goods. Consequently, cash flow problems surfaced, and GreenWave was in danger of going bankrupt. Ryan was aware of the consequences of his choices and the chance that his dream may not come true.

Reaching Out to His HBS Network: Ryan sought assistance from his HBS network at this crucial time. He asked classmates, mentors, and past instructors for input. Ryan gained fresh ideas and possible answers from their varied viewpoints and combined expertise. Inspired by their backing, he made the decision to revamp

GreenWave's business plan and look for further capital.

Pivoting the Business Model: Ryan came to the realization that he had to change the business model in order to save GreenWave. He changed the emphasis from just providing fish to collaborating with eateries and merchants that were as committed to sustainability as GreenWave was. With this tactical change, GreenWave was able to establish enduring bonds with important partners and guarantee consistent sources of income.

Securing Funding and Support: Ryan sought investors with newfound confidence after revising his business proposal. He openly discussed the difficulties GreenWave has encountered and the lessons discovered. Investors were struck by his candor and his clear vision for GreenWave's future development and impact. Ryan was able to raise more money, which gave the company the resources it needed to grow and stabilize.

Operational Overhaul: Ryan understood that long-term success at GreenWave depended on streamlining the company's operations. In order to boost productivity, he concentrated on investing in technology, enhancing supply chain management, and simplifying procedures. Ryan also gave recruiting seasoned experts who contributed significant knowledge to the team top priority. These modifications improved GreenWave's operating capacities and set up the business for long-term success.

Marketing and Brand Repositioning: Ryan started a thorough marketing effort that emphasized GreenWave's dedication to sustainability, innovation, and excellence in order to restore the company's brand. In order to establish a connection with the audience, he told tales about GreenWave's history and the purpose of ocean conservation. The target market responded well to this genuine approach, which restored faith in and interest in GreenWave's offerings.

Community Engagement and Advocacy: Ryan also gave attention to these two areas. He utilized social media, industry events, and partnerships with environmental groups to spread the word about sustainable seafood. Ryan established GreenWave as a leader in the sustainability movement and cultivated a devoted clientele that backed the business's objectives by speaking out in favor of sustainability.

The Turnaround Success: The tale of GreenWave's turnaround is proof of the strength of adaptation, resilience, and strategic thinking. The business not only overcame its early difficulties under Ryan's direction, but it also came out stronger and more significant. GreenWave's creative approach to aquaculture was recognized, and the business was able to sign deals with significant retailers and restaurant chains.

Awards and Recognition: GreenWave received recognition for its achievements. For its efforts to promote environmentally conscious practices and sustainable seafood, the firm was recognized with many honors. These honors increased GreenWave's standing and prominence in the sector, drawing in new clients and partners.

Long-Term Impact: In the seafood sector, GreenWave is now recognized as a symbol of sustainability and innovation. Beyond GreenWave, other companies have been influenced by the company's activities to embrace more environmentally friendly methods. Ryan's story of almost failing and then building a successful business serves as a potent reminder that obstacles and setbacks can be used as stepping stones to achievement.

Final Thoughts

Overcoming obstacles and setbacks is a crucial aspect of the entrepreneurial path. The significance of resilience, adaptation, and strategic decision-making is emphasized by Emily's experience with TechGenius and Ryan's success story with GreenWave. Both entrepreneurs overcame substantial challenges and succeeded by using their Harvard Business School degrees and learning from their failures.

With proper preparation and a proactive approach, common startup problems, including not doing market research, having insufficient financial planning, growing quickly, and disregarding criticism, may be avoided. Developing a development attitude, honestly assessing setbacks, looking for mentoring, and emphasizing iterative progress are crucial tactics for transforming obstacles into opportunities.

As you go on your own entrepreneurial path, keep in mind that failure is a necessary learning experience rather than the end. Remain devoted to your goal, be flexible in your thinking, and take advantage of the advice and connections in your network. By doing this, you may get over obstacles, steer clear of typical traps, and eventually realize the full potential of your business. Welcome to the exciting world of business, where every setback can be used as a springboard for success and every obstacle may be seen as a chance for personal development.

CHAPTER 10

TECHNOLOGY'S FUNCTION IN STARTUPS

Using Technology to Gain a Competitive Edge

Technology has completely changed the way entrepreneurs work by offering platforms and tools that greatly increase productivity, scalability, and creativity. Knowing how to use technology to your advantage as an entrepreneur might be the difference between success and failure. Let's examine the tale of Julia, a Harvard Business School alumna who started HealthConnect, a firm that aims to incorporate technology into healthcare services, to better understand this.

Spotting the Opportunity: Julia's journey started with the basic realization that patients often found it difficult to get timely and accurate health information due to the fragmented nature of the healthcare system. Julia recognized an opportunity to close this gap between healthcare and technology, so she built a platform that combined different healthcare services—from telemedicine to patient records—into a single, easily navigable interface.

Building the Tech Infrastructure: Julia realized early on that HealthConnect's success depended on having a strong tech infrastructure. She made an investment in cloud computing to guarantee data protection and scalability. Julia also collaborated with top IT companies to create a safe and smooth platform. HealthConnect's ability to manage massive data sets and provide real-time updates—both crucial for patients and healthcare providers—was made possible by this foundation.

Using Data Analytics: The capacity to gather and examine enormous volumes of data is one of technology's main benefits. Julia used data analytics to learn more about the behaviors of her patients, the effectiveness of her treatments, and the efficiency of her operations. HealthConnect may be able to better serve customers, spot patterns, and tailor healthcare recommendations by evaluating this data. In addition to improving patient care, this data-driven strategy gave HealthConnect a competitive advantage.

Embracing Mobile Technology: Julia saw the value of mobile technology in expanding access to healthcare as cellphones became increasingly popular. She created a smartphone app that lets users schedule appointments, see medical histories, and communicate with physicians. This ease of use was revolutionary, especially for patients who were in isolated locations or had limited mobility. HealthConnect's mobile app swiftly rose to prominence as one of its most well-liked features.

Putting Artificial Intelligence (AI) into Practice: Julia was also a pioneer in the use of AI. She added artificial intelligence (AI) to HealthConnect's platform so that patients could have virtual health assistants who could book appointments, respond to questions, and even make an initial diagnosis based on symptoms. By cutting down on wait times and offering immediate assistance, this not only increased efficiency but also improved the patient experience.

Harvard Perspectives on Technology Inclusion

Students at Harvard Business School get state-of-the-art advice on how to successfully incorporate technology into company strategies. Several important ideas Julia learned at HBS influenced her work with HealthConnect.

Strategic Alignment: The significance of coordinating technology with the overarching company strategy is a crucial takeaway from HBS. Julia made sure that HealthConnect's technological initiatives all supported the organization's goal of enhancing patient care. The company's objectives were better served by prioritizing IT investments that were in line with this strategic alignment.

Cross-functional cooperation: In tech integration, HBS highlights the need for cross-functional cooperation. Julia promoted a collaborative atmosphere among the IT team at HealthConnect and medical professionals. This partnership made sure that the technology created was useful, easy to use, and addressed actual healthcare issues. It also made it easier for new technology to be adopted by the whole company.

Ongoing Education and Adjustment: Since technology is always changing, HBS emphasizes the need for ongoing education and adjustment. Julia promoted a culture of innovation and constant development, which helped HealthConnect stay at the forefront of technological breakthroughs. She made sure her staff members were up to speed on the newest trends and technology by giving them the opportunity for continuous training and development.

Customer-Centric Approach: Keeping a customer-centric approach to IT integration is another important takeaway from HBS. Involving patients and healthcare professionals in the development process, Julia solicited input and made incremental changes in response to their requirements. This strategy guaranteed that HealthConnect's technological solutions were useful and efficient while also improving customer happiness.

Risk Management: There are hazards associated with technological integration, including data breaches and system malfunctions. The value of risk management in tech integration is something that HBS teaches. To reduce hazards, Julia put strict cybersecurity safeguards into place and created backup plans. In order to guarantee the dependability and security of the platform, she also carried out regular audits and stress testing.

Case Study: [Founder 9] and Their Tech-Driven Success

In order to elucidate the transformational potential of technology in businesses, let us examine the experiences of David, a fellow HBS alumnus who established AgriTech Solutions, an organization using technology to revolutionize agriculture.

The Vision: David was raised in a rural area and saw firsthand the difficulties farmers have, such as erratic weather patterns and ineffective resource management. He had an idea for a firm that would utilize technology to solve these issues and raise agricultural production after he graduated from HBS. Hence, AgriTech Solutions was established.

Creating Smart Farming Tools: David's first course of action was creating tools for smart farming that would assist farmers in making data-driven choices. He developed a line of Internet of Things (IoT) sensors that kept an eye on crop health, temperature, and soil moisture. Farmers were able to maximize crop yields, minimize water use, and improve irrigation by using the real-time data these devices supplied. Smart farming equipment became popular, and farmers soon realized how technology might improve their operations.

Using AI and Big Data: David saw how these technologies may revolutionize agriculture. He created an AI-powered platform that examined previous crop performance, weather predictions, and data from IoT sensors. With the use of predictive analytics from the platform, farmers were able to foresee and reduce risks like insect infestations and crop illnesses. AgriTech Solutions gave farmers the ability to make proactive and knowledgeable choices by using big data and AI.

Implementing Blockchain for Transparency: David included blockchain technology in AgriTech Solutions to solve concerns with traceability and transparency in the food supply chain. The produce's path from farm to table was monitored by blockchain technology, giving customers comprehensive information about the treatment and provenance of their food. In addition to fostering customer trust, this openness assisted farmers in obtaining higher prices for their goods.

Expanding to Precision Agriculture: David also made the move into precision agriculture, giving farmers comprehensive insights into their farms via the use of drones and satellite photography. The instruments for precision agriculture assisted farmers in identifying problem regions, such as poorly performing parts of a field. Farmers might decrease resource waste and increase overall output by taking quick action on these problems.

Empowering and Educating Farmers: David recognized that assistance and education were necessary for the use of technology. He set up support facilities and training courses to assist farmers in comprehending and making the most of AgriTech Solutions' offerings. David made sure farmers could make full use of technology by providing them with information and tools.

Creating Strategic Partnerships: David formed strategic alliances with IT firms, government agencies, and agricultural groups in order to grow AgriTech Solutions. Through these alliances, AgriTech Solutions was able to get capital, access to new markets, and technical know-how. Working with well-established organizations gave the business legitimacy and sped up its expansion.

Achieving Global Impact: AgriTech Solutions' cutting-edge approach to agriculture immediately brought it acclaim. Farmers all around the globe, from tiny family farms to major agricultural conglomerates, have embraced the company's technologies. David changed millions of lives when his idea of using technology to enhance agricultural methods and guarantee food security came to pass.

Awards and Recognition: David received recognition for his work with AgriTech Solutions. For its contributions to technical innovation and sustainable agriculture, the firm was recognized with many honors. These honors improved AgriTech Solutions' standing even further and led to new prospects.

Overcoming Difficulties: There were difficulties along the way. Technical difficulties, governmental restrictions, and opposition from established agricultural communities confronted David. Nevertheless, he overcame these obstacles with the support of his willpower and the knowledge he gained at HBS. David was able to convert challenges into opportunities by maintaining his mission-focused concentration and making adjustments for shifting conditions.

AgriTech Solutions' Future: In the present, AgriTech Solutions keeps expanding the frontiers of agricultural technology. The business is experimenting with cutting-edge technologies, including genetic editing, autonomous agricultural equipment, and vertical farming. AgriTech Solutions will continue to lead the agricultural revolution because of David's dedication to sustainability and innovation.

Final Thoughts

Without a doubt, technology plays a revolutionary role in startups by providing chances for innovation, growth, and competitive advantage. David's success with AgriTech

Solutions and Julia's path with HealthConnect serve as examples of how technology can propel businesses forward and have a significant effect.

Strategic alignment, cross-functional cooperation, ongoing learning, a customer-centric mindset, and good risk management are all necessary for using technology successfully. Through the integration of these concepts, entrepreneurs may fully use technology to surmount obstacles and accomplish their objectives.

When you set out on your entrepreneurial path, keep in mind that technology is an effective instrument that may help your firm achieve unprecedented success. Leverage the knowledge and resources at your disposal, embrace innovation, and maintain your adaptability. By doing this, you may create a tech-driven business that changes the world while also succeeding. Greetings from the vibrant and fascinating world of technology companies, where the opportunities are endless and each obstacle offers a chance to advance.

CHAPTER 11

THE VIEW FROM A GLOBAL ANGLE

Extending Across Boundaries

There has never been a better chance for businesses to grow outside of their native markets than there is in the connected world of today. A company's competitive edge may be strengthened, new income streams can be generated, and business risks can be diversified through international growth. But expanding internationally also brings with it special difficulties that require careful planning, cultural awareness, and in-depth knowledge of regional markets.

Let's examine the background of Alex, a Harvard Business School alumnus who started EcoSolutions, a business committed to offering sustainable energy solutions, in order to better understand the complexities of international growth.

The Vision for Global Impact: Alex set out on a quest to provide accessible, sustainable energy solutions in order to fight climate change. Offering cutting-edge solar panels and energy storage devices, EcoSolutions began as a little firm in the US. Alex soon saw that entering foreign areas where access to renewable energy was scarce would greatly increase the influence of EcoSolutions.

Identifying Global Opportunities: Selecting the appropriate markets was the initial move in EcoSolutions' international growth. In order to identify nations with strong demand for sustainable energy, advantageous regulatory frameworks, and encouraging governmental policies, Alex and his colleagues carried out a thorough investigation. They identified a number of prospective areas where there was an urgent need for dependable and sustainable energy solutions, such as Southeast Asia, Africa, and South America.

Creating Local Partnerships: Alex placed a high priority on forming reliable alliances with regional businesses, governmental bodies, and nonprofits since he recognized that having local knowledge is essential for successful foreign growth. EcoSolutions gained important insights into regional market dynamics, legal requirements, and customer preferences as a result of these relationships. In order to overcome cultural barriers and foster trust in the communities they sought to serve, EcoSolutions also benefited from working with regional partners.

Adapting to Local Markets: Creating goods and services that cater to regional demands is one of the main obstacles to global business expansion. The products offered by EcoSolutions were tailored by Alex and his group to each target market's particular requirements. For example, they created autonomous solar energy systems that might function in areas with inadequate grid infrastructure. They focused on scalable systems that could be readily extended as required in regions with high energy demand. Gaining credibility and traction in new areas required this flexibility.

Navigating Regulatory Landscapes: Standards and regulations pertaining to energy goods vary by nation. Alex understood how crucial it was to comprehend and abide by these rules in order to prevent delays and legal problems. EcoSolutions used consultants and legal specialists in the area to make sure that their goods fulfilled all required requirements and certifications. In addition to making market entrance easier, this proactive strategy reaffirmed EcoSolutions' commitment to quality and compliance.

Cultural Sensitivity and Communication: Cultural variations have a big influence on how well businesses do internationally. Within his team, Alex stressed the need for good communication and cultural awareness. EcoSolutions made an investment in cultural training initiatives to teach staff members about the norms, principles, and business etiquette of the areas they were expanding into. Because of their cultural sensitivity, EcoSolutions was able to establish trusting bonds with regional stakeholders and steer clear of misconceptions that would have impeded their progress.

Harvard Techniques for Global Marketplaces

Students at Harvard Business School get tools to help them navigate the challenges of global marketplaces. Numerous important insights that Alex learned at HBS shaped his strategy for expanding internationally.

Market entrance strategies: HBS offers courses on a range of market entrance techniques, including wholly-owned subsidiaries, joint ventures, exporting, and franchising. Alex assessed every choice to find the best course of action for EcoSolutions in various marketplaces. The quickest path to market in certain areas was to create joint ventures with local businesses; in other areas, however, creating wholly-owned subsidiaries gave firms more flexibility and control.

Global Value Networks: Improving the efficacy and cost-efficiency of the supply chain requires a thorough understanding of global value networks. Alex created a worldwide value chain map for EcoSolutions, pinpointing important vendors, production locations, and delivery routes. EcoSolutions lowered costs and strengthened supply chain resilience by carefully placing manufacturing facilities and, if feasible, procuring resources locally.

Risk Management: There are a number of dangers associated with expanding internationally, such as market volatility, currency fluctuations, and political unpredictability. The significance of risk management in international business is emphasized by HBS. Alex created all-encompassing risk management plans that included currency risk hedging, regional investment diversification, and keeping tabs on geopolitical events. By taking these steps, EcoSolutions was able to reduce risks and keep its global operations stable.

Global Leadership: Managing a multinational company calls for a certain set of abilities. Global leadership, which encompasses managing cross-cultural teams, cultivating a diverse and inclusive company culture, and leading with a global mentality, is emphasized at HBS. Alex accepted these ideas and made sure that people with a variety of experiences from abroad were involved in the leadership team of EcoSolutions. This variety improved decision-making and made the business more capable of navigating challenging international issues.

Sustainability and Corporate Responsibility: In the current international business climate, establishing a solid reputation and winning over stakeholders' confidence depend heavily on sustainability and corporate responsibility. The significance of incorporating sustainability into corporate strategy is taught at HBS. By offering sustainable energy solutions, lowering the company's carbon footprint, adhering to ethical business practices, and supporting social projects that benefit the community, Alex elevated sustainability to the top of EcoSolutions' worldwide growth pillars.

Case Study: [Founder 10] and Their Global Expansion

Let's examine the path of Maya, an additional HBS alumni who started FreshHarvest, a business dedicated to offering sustainable and organic food items, in order to better highlight the concepts of worldwide growth.

The Inspiration and Mission: Maya founded FreshHarvest because she is passionate about sustainable agriculture and a healthy lifestyle. The company's goal was to increase global consumer access to organic and sustainably sourced food. In its early years, FreshHarvest was a tiny business in California that sold packaged foods and organic vegetables at neighborhood farmers' markets and online. But Maya quickly understood that FreshHarvest needed to go worldwide in order to have a meaningful influence on the world's food systems.

Assessing Market Potential: Maya started by determining the potential markets for sustainable and organic food items in various areas. Because of the increasing demand for organic food and the high level of consumer knowledge about sustainability, she listed Europe, Japan, and certain regions of the Middle East as high-potential areas. Maya's group carried out in-depth market research, examining local regulations, competitive markets, and customer preferences.

Entering European Markets: One of Maya's first global growth goals for FreshHarvest was Europe. The strict requirements set by the European Union for organic certification matched FreshHarvest's dedication to sustainability and high quality. Maya established a subsidiary in Germany that functioned as a center for product distribution across Europe. In order to obtain extra produce and guarantee that their goods fulfilled the high standards of freshness and quality set by European customers, FreshHarvest also worked with nearby organic farms.

Navigating Japan's Market: Due to cultural differences and customer preferences, expanding into Japan faced special hurdles. In food goods, Japanese customers place a high value on authenticity, quality, and trust. Maya collaborated extensively with regional specialists to comprehend these subtleties and modify FreshHarvest's branding and promotional tactics correspondingly. The business prioritized openness, emphasizing its dedication to sustainable methods and farm-to-table philosophy. Additionally, FreshHarvest established a flagship location in Tokyo so that customers could meet the company and discover its principles.

Taking on the Middle East: The Middle East had encouraging prospects but needed cautious maneuvering because of differing laws and market circumstances. Maya focused on wealthy regions where demand for organic and healthful foods was rising, such as Saudi Arabia and the United Arab Emirates. In order to reach customers who were concerned about their health, FreshHarvest partnered with upscale stores and online platforms. Additionally, the business modified its product line to include things like organic dates and spices that fit regional dietary requirements and tastes.

Logistics and Supply Chain Management: One of FreshHarvest's biggest challenges was overseeing supply chains and logistics in many different locations. Maya put in place an advanced supply chain management system that made it possible to monitor shipments, inventories, and quality assurance in real time. FreshHarvest preserved the quality and freshness of its goods via effective distribution and logistics optimization, which was essential for keeping customers' confidence.

Cultural Adaptation and Local Engagement: FreshHarvest's success was largely attributed to its capacity for both local community engagement and cultural adaptation. Maya gave special attention to employing local people who were familiar with the customs and business environment of each area. Additionally, FreshHarvest participated in community projects, including promoting regional organic farming methods and holding courses on sustainable living. These initiatives strengthened FreshHarvest's ties to regional stakeholders and reaffirmed the company's dedication to having a good social effect.

Overcoming Regulatory Obstacles: FreshHarvest had difficulties as a result of the various regulatory requirements that each location has for food items. Maya's team collaborated extensively with regulatory bodies to guarantee adherence to all mandatory certifications and standards. This proactive strategy reduced delays caused by regulations and made market entry easier. FreshHarvest gained the trust of authorities and customers by showcasing their dedication to quality and compliance.

Creating a Worldwide Brand: Maya realized that a compelling value proposition and consistent messaging were essential to creating a worldwide brand. FreshHarvest placed a strong emphasis on sustainability, openness, and excellence in its branding. In order to establish a connection with customers, the firm shared the tale of their goods' journey from farm to table and emphasized the advantages of sustainable agriculture. Customers all across the globe were drawn to FreshHarvest by its genuine and well-coordinated brand story, which set it apart from rivals.

The Outcomes and Implications: FreshHarvest's international growth was a huge success. In each of its target areas, the business rapidly built a devoted clientele, and revenues skyrocketed. Due to the items' placement in prestigious retail chains, internet portals, and niche markets, a larger consumer base now has access to organic and sustainable food. The company's influence went beyond its financial performance since FreshHarvest encourage healthy living, supported environmentally friendly agricultural methods, and lessened its effect on the environment.

Future Growth and Innovation: With an eye toward the future, Maya is looking into fresh markets and creative methods to broaden

FreshHarvest's reach internationally. To increase production and sustainability, the firm is investing in cutting-edge agricultural technology, including precision agriculture and vertical farming. In order to solve the issues surrounding global food security and advance sustainable food systems, FreshHarvest is also looking into forming alliances with foreign groups.

CHAPTER 12

MORAL BUSINESS PRACTICES

The Value of Morality in Business

The quest for innovation and financial gain often takes center stage in the world of startups. But ethical entrepreneurship is just as important since it shapes a company's legacy and social effect in addition to its profitability. Prioritizing ethics helps entrepreneurs create a healthy corporate culture, gain the confidence of stakeholders, and advance society.

The Moral Compass: The desire to meet a need or find a solution to an issue often drives the beginning of an entrepreneur's journey. There are moments when the demands of profitability and scale eclipse this admirable aim. But it's crucial to have a strong moral compass. Making moral choices may pay off in the long run by fostering staff happiness, customer loyalty, and sustainable development.

Building an Integrity Culture: An ethical company begins with an integrity culture. Setting clear norms and ideals, as well as demonstrating moral conduct, is how leaders set the tone. Every facet of the company is impacted by this culture, from marketing and customer service to decision-making and product creation. Employees are more inclined to respect ethics in their own jobs when they see that their bosses place a high priority on it.

Ethics and Innovation: Ethical issues may spur innovation in addition to just preventing damage. Businesses that put sustainability first, for instance, often set the standard for innovative techniques and technology that improve both the bottom line and the environment. Thinking beyond the next big thing and taking the wider picture into account while doing business is encouraged by ethical entrepreneurship.

Harvard's Social Responsibility Philosophy

The Harvard Business School (HBS) has always acknowledged the value of social responsibility and ethics in business education. These values are ingrained in HBS students, equipping them to lead with integrity and have a good influence in their fields.

The HBS Ethical Framework: Case studies, debates, and real-world applications are how ethics are included in the curriculum at HBS.

Pupils get experience navigating difficult moral conundrums and comprehending the effects of their choices. Creating a comprehensive viewpoint that takes into account the interests of all parties involved—including workers, clients, communities, and the environment—is the main goal.

Leadership and Ethics: HBS emphasizes that moral leadership is leading by example and motivating others to act morally, rather than just adhering to the law. Leaders need to be open, responsible, and prepared to make tough decisions that put the greater good ahead of temporary benefits. This strategy cultivates an environment in which morality and commercial success go hand in hand.

Social Impact Activities: Community service, social businesses, and sustainability projects are just a few of the social impact activities Harvard encourages its students to participate in. These stories provide useful advice on how companies might solve environmental and social issues while still turning a profit. Alumni from Harvard Business School are often at the vanguard of movements that promote good change, proving the importance of morality and social responsibility in business.

Case Study: [Founder 11] and Their Ethical Business Model

Let's look at Samira's story, an HBS alumni who started CleanGreen, an eco-friendly cleaning product firm, to demonstrate the tenets of ethical entrepreneurship.

The Inspiration: Samira's involvement in a project at HBS aimed at lowering plastic waste sparked her interest in sustainability. She became aware of the detrimental impacts that traditional cleaning supplies had on the environment and human health. Samira was determined to change things, so she imagined a business that provided eco-friendly, safe, and efficient cleaning products.

Establishing CleanGreen: Following her graduation, Samira established CleanGreen with the specific goal of producing non-toxic, biodegradable cleaning products packed with environmentally friendly materials. Among the many obstacles she had to overcome were increased manufacturing costs and doubts from possible investors. Samira remained focused nonetheless, because of her unyielding adherence to her principles.

Creating an Ethical Supply Chain: Establishing an ethical supply chain was one of Samira's top goals. She purchased raw materials from vendors that followed fair trade and sustainability standards. Due to CleanGreen's dedication to ethical sourcing, its goods were not only consumer-safe but also promoted environmental stewardship and moral labor standards.

Transparent Marketing: CleanGreen's marketing approach was based on transparency. Samira thought that customers had a right to know the precise contents of the items they used. The components and their origins were listed on CleanGreen's packaging in an honest and straightforward manner. In order to create a community of knowledgeable and ethical customers, the business also taught clients about how their decisions affected the environment.

Employee Welfare: Samira understood that her team members were CleanGreen's core. She put into effect regulations that guaranteed equitable pay, secure working environments, and chances for advancement in the workforce. Samira built a devoted and driven workforce committed to the company's goal by establishing a welcoming and inclusive work environment.

Community Engagement: CleanGreen acted as a catalyst for education and community involvement in addition to being a company. Samira started campaigns to encourage sustainable living and increase public knowledge of environmental challenges. CleanGreen organized seminars and educational programs in collaboration with local groups and educational institutions to encourage individuals to make environmentally responsible decisions on a daily basis.

Navigating Challenges: There were roadblocks along the way to success. CleanGreen had to continuously innovate in order to keep ahead of the competition, which included well-known companies. When compared to less ethical rivals, Samira's dedication to ethics sometimes resulted in greater expenses and slower development. She didn't waver, however, since she thought moral behavior would eventually make the company stronger and more robust.

The Impact of Ethical Decisions: CleanGreen started to reap the benefits of its moral decisions. The business attracted a devoted clientele that admired its dedication to sustainability and openness. Major retail chains carried

CleanGreen's goods, which won praise for their excellence and environmental effect. Samira distinguished her brand in a saturated market by putting ethics first.

Expanding the Vision: Samira's vision expanded together with CleanGreen. She made research and development investments to produce new goods that tackled more environmental issues. In an effort to decrease plastic waste, CleanGreen launched a range of refillable goods. To guarantee that packaging materials were handled appropriately, the company collaborated with recycling initiatives.

A Trajectory of Ethical Guidance: Samira's influence went beyond CleanGreen. She started giving talks at conferences and coaching aspiring business owners as an advocate for moral entrepreneurship. Her narrative demonstrated that success could be attained without sacrificing morals, and it encouraged others to place a higher priority on ethics in their own endeavors.

Acknowledgement and Awards: CleanGreen has received a great deal of attention and recognition due to its dedication to sustainability and ethics. The business was praised for its cutting-edge goods, moral business conduct, and beneficial effects on the environment and local communities. Samira was further convinced by these honors that being an ethical entrepreneur was not just the moral thing to do but also a successful and fulfilling business plan.

Future Objectives: Samira has big ambitions for CleanGreen in the future. She wants to access new markets, increase the company's product offering, and keep pushing the envelope on sustainability. Samira is dedicated to promoting laws and procedures that encourage ethical corporate conduct in order to further the discourse on ethical entrepreneurship.

Final Thoughts

In addition to being a moral requirement, ethical entrepreneurship may be a competitive advantage that promotes long-term success and beneficial outcomes. Samira's experience with CleanGreen serves as an example of how a firm commitment to ethics can set a business apart, win over stakeholders, and provide long-term value.

The approach to ethics and social responsibility taken by Harvard Business School gives entrepreneurs the knowledge and skills they need to successfully negotiate the challenging environment of contemporary business. Integrating ethical values into their plans allows entrepreneurs to motivate their teams, lead with integrity, and have a positive impact on a more sustainable and equitable world.

Remember that every choice you make as you set out on your entrepreneurial journey will have an influence on society and the direction your company will take. Adopting the tenets of ethical entrepreneurship will lead to success and a lasting legacy of constructive transformation. Greetings from the realm of ethical entrepreneurship, where success in business is based on your principles and doing good goes hand in hand with prosperity.

CHAPTER 13

LONG-TERM GOALS AND STRATEGIES FOR LIVING

Future Planning: Scaling or Selling

Future planning is an essential part of the business development process for each entrepreneur. Having a long-term vision is critical, regardless of your objective—growing your company into a multinational corporation or getting it ready for a smooth departure. In addition to directing your strategic choices, this vision makes sure that your company is robust and sustainable in the face of adversity.

The Fork in the Road: When a startup expands, its founders often have to choose between growing the company or getting ready to leave. To remain competitive, scaling entails growing operations, breaking into new markets, and constantly innovating. Conversely, an out-of-business acquisition, merger, or initial public offering (IPO) are examples of exit strategies. The decision is based on the founder's objectives, the success of the business, and the state of the market. Each route offers a unique set of possibilities and problems.

Scaling: Building for the Long Haul: Talented employees, a strong infrastructure, and a well-defined vision are necessary for a company to grow. In order to guarantee sustainable development that is in line with the goals and values of the organization, strategic planning is required. For instance, entrepreneurs need to think about how to grow production or services while maintaining quality and consumer happiness. In order to scale effectively, supply chains must be optimized, technology must be leveraged, and enough finance must be obtained to support expansion projects.

The Role of Innovation: Scaling a firm requires constant innovation. Businesses need to innovate and enhance their current offerings in order to stay ahead of customer preferences and market trends. This calls for a creative culture and a readiness to take measured chances. An effective scaling plan must include spending money on R&D, paying attention to user input, and encouraging an innovative culture.

Getting Ready for an Exit: In order to optimize the value of their company, entrepreneurs must carefully consider whether an exit strategy is their objective. This includes making certain that the company's finances are in order, that legal and regulatory compliance is maintained, and that its operations are optimized. Finding possible partners or purchasers and presenting the business as an appealing acquisition target are further steps in the exit preparation process. This might include promoting the business's distinctive value offering, growing the clientele, and fortifying the brand.

Harvard Views on Profitable Exits

Harvard Business School's substantial research and case studies provide insightful information on effective departure plans. These tips assist business owners in navigating the challenges of closing a company and getting the results they want.

Understanding Market Dynamics: A crucial takeaway from HBS is the significance of comprehending the timing and dynamics of the market. When the market is favorable and the firm is in a solid position, successful exits often happen. This necessitates keeping up with economic developments, industry trends, and prospective changes to the competitive environment. Entrepreneurs with the ability to foresee shifts and behave strategically have a higher chance of having successful exits.

Building a Strong Foundation: Prior to thinking about a departure, HBS stresses the need to lay a solid foundation. This entails possessing a strong company plan, a devoted clientele, and a history of steady expansion and financial success. Prospective investors and purchasers find companies with stability and growth prospects more appealing.

Selecting the Appropriate Departure Strategy: Different departure methods are possible, and each has consequences of its own. According to HBS, the objectives of the founder, the company's stage of growth, and the state of the market all play a role in selecting the best exit plan. Typical departure tactics consist of:

Acquisition: The business is sold to a bigger organization. In addition to instant cash gains, this may provide access to more resources and networks.

merger: uniting with another business to form a more powerful firm. Both market presence and operational efficiency may benefit from this.

First Public Offering (IPO): getting listed and offering shares for sale to the general public. This entails market constraints and regulatory complications, yet it may generate a substantial amount of funding and boost visibility.

Management Buyout (MBO): Transferring ownership of the business to the current management group. This may guarantee continuity and protect the values and culture of the business.

Valuation and Negotiation: HBS emphasizes the significance of valuation and negotiation in the departure process. The founders need to be well aware of the worth of their firm and ready to bargain for conditions that support their objectives. To make sure that the terms of the agreement are advantageous and safeguard the interests of all parties involved, this entails collaborating with financial consultants, legal specialists, and other experts.

Case Study: [Founder 12] and Their Exit Strategy

Let's examine the path of Ben, an HBS graduate who built TechSolutions, a business that created cutting-edge software solutions for the healthcare sector, to highlight the concepts of long-term vision and exit strategy.

The Beginning: Ben's journey started with a strong interest in healthcare and technology. He started TechSolutions with the goal of using cutting-edge technologies to transform healthcare after receiving his degree from HBS. A cloud-based platform that facilitated patient data administration, better provider-to-provider communication, and improved patient outcomes was the company's main offering.

Building the Business: TechSolutions attracted a growing clientele of hospitals, clinics, and healthcare providers as it rapidly gained momentum in the healthcare sector. Ben made strategic alliances, investments in customer support, and product development with the goal of creating a solid basis. The business distinguished itself from rivals and became a leader in the sector because of its dedication to innovation and quality.

Scaling the Business: Ben had to tackle the task of growing TechSolutions to satisfy growing customer demand. He hired more people, set up more offices, and ventured into other markets. In order to improve the platform's capabilities, Ben additionally made investments in cutting-edge technology like data analytics and artificial intelligence. TechSolutions was able to satisfy the changing demands of healthcare providers and remain ahead of market trends because of its ongoing innovation.

Ready for a departure: Following years of expansion, Ben started thinking about his departure plan. Selling the business, in his opinion, would free up the capital required to advance TechSolutions and increase its influence in the healthcare sector. Ben made sure that the platform was scalable, the company's operations were effective, and the financials were in order while he methodically got ready to go.

Identifying Potential Buyers: Ben identified a number of possible purchasers, including private equity groups and bigger healthcare technology businesses. In order to guarantee that

TechSolutions' objective would be maintained, he concentrated on purchasing from clients that shared those goals and beliefs. Ben had conversations with a number of people, considering their offerings and strategic alignment.

Bargaining and Deal Structure: Following a careful assessment, Ben made the decision to sell TechSolutions to a top healthcare technology business that was dedicated to advancing the platform's advancement and saw its potential. Comprehensive talks about post-acquisition integration, deal structure, and value were part of the negotiating process. Ben made sure the conditions of the sale were advantageous and in line with his objectives by carefully collaborating with financial and legal consultants.

The Exit: TechSolutions' purchase was a noteworthy turning point. Ben and his group reaped significant financial benefits from the transaction, and TechSolutions was well-positioned for future expansion and innovation thanks to the purchasing company's network and resources. Additionally, the purchase guaranteed that TechSolutions' clients would get access to new and improved capabilities and support.

Post-Exit Involvement: Ben continued to serve as a strategic adviser for TechSolutions after the purchase. This made it possible for him to carry on advancing the goals of the business and guarantee a seamless transfer. Ben's guidance and proficiency played a crucial role in assimilating TechSolutions into the broader enterprise and propelling its sustained prosperity.

Takeaways: For business owners organizing their own departures, Ben's experience provides insightful takeaways. He highlights the significance of:

Having a Clear Vision: Strategic choices are guided by a long-term vision that positions the organization for future growth.

Building a Strong Foundation: Attracting new customers requires a strong company concept, a devoted clientele, and steady development.

Meticulously Preparing: A seamless withdrawal process depends on making sure that the operations, finances, and legal issues are in order.

Selecting the Correct Partner: Ensuring the business's survival requires finding a buyer who shares the company's mission and values.

Staying active: Continuing to be active in the company after a departure may help ensure a smooth transition and promote continued success.

Final Thoughts

Preparing for the future is an essential part of being an entrepreneur, whether it involves growth or an exit strategy. Harvard Business School offers insightful advice and practical tactics to assist business owners in navigating these difficult choices and coming up with winning solutions. Through comprehension of market dynamics, the establishment of a robust foundation, and the selection of an appropriate exit plan, entrepreneurs may optimize the worth of their enterprises and generate enduring influence.

Ben's experience with TechSolutions serves as an excellent example of both successful exits and long-term vision. His dedication to strategic planning, innovation, and moral leadership made sure TechSolutions not only achieved financial success but also had a significant influence on the healthcare sector. As you reflect on your own business career, keep in mind that making plans for the future involves more than simply maximizing profits—it also entails leaving a lasting legacy of constructive change and steady expansion.

CHAPTER 14

BALANCING WORK AND LIFE

Achieving Harmony Between Work and Life

Long hours, unrelenting attention, and a steadfast dedication to the company are often characteristics of the entrepreneurial path. This extreme commitment, nevertheless, may have a price if it causes burnout and disregard for one's own needs. Achieving work-life balance is crucial for the startup's long-term success as well as the health of the entrepreneur. In order to achieve true harmony, one must balance one's personal and professional goals without sacrificing the other.

The Myth of the 24/7 Hustle: There is a

common misconception about entrepreneurs: they labor nonstop, get by on little sleep, and never take a vacation. Although diligence and commitment are important, this misconception often elevates an unsustainable way of living. Persistent overwork may result in diminished productivity, burnout, and poor decision-making. Successful business people, on the other hand, understand how important it is to strike a balance between work and personal obligations in order to refresh and regenerate.

Setting Boundaries: Establishing distinct boundaries between one's personal and professional lives is a crucial first step in establishing work-life balance. This entails setting aside certain times and locations for work while giving family, friends, and hobbies equal priority. Entrepreneurs may keep work from invading every part of their lives and stay connected to what really matters by establishing boundaries.

Making Self-Care a Priority: Keeping balance is mostly dependent on self-care. This involves having a balanced diet, getting enough sleep, exercising often, and making time for hobbies and leisure. These are not hedonistic pursuits; rather, they are essential to preserving one's bodily and mental well-being. Self-sufficient entrepreneurs are better able to manage their businesses' needs and make wiser judgments.

Mindfulness and Stress Management: Entrepreneurs may reduce stress and stay focused by engaging in mindfulness exercises like yoga and meditation. Emotional control and resilience may be enhanced by these techniques, which promote awareness and presence. Entrepreneurs may better manage the stress of operating a company and maintain their composure by implementing mindfulness into their daily practices.

Harvard Advice on Keeping Your Balance

The Harvard Business School understands the value of work-life balance and provides a number of tools to assist entrepreneurs in successfully juggling their personal and professional obligations. These tactics are supported by research and the practical experience of successful company executives.

Time Management: Achieving balance requires effective time management. To keep organized, this entails prioritizing chores, assigning them to others, and using tools like calendars and to-do lists. Entrepreneurs who are skilled at time management may make sure they set aside enough time for both business and leisure pursuits.

Delegation and Trust: An entrepreneur's workload may be reduced by assigning responsibilities to team members and having faith in them. Entrepreneurs may concentrate on making strategic choices and dedicate time to personal interests by assembling a competent and trustworthy staff, freeing them from the continual stress of managing their firm.

Flexible Work Arrangements: A better work-life balance may also be facilitated by flexible work arrangements. This might be reduced workweeks, flexible scheduling, or remote work choices. Entrepreneurs who embrace flexibility are able to balance corporate goals with personal obligations.

Disconnecting from Work: It's critical for business owners to take frequent breaks from their jobs. This entails setting aside time for vacations and getaways from electronic gadgets. Disconnecting on a regular basis encourages creativity and new insights while returning to work, as well as preventing burnout.

Support Systems: It's critical to have robust support networks in place. This includes peer, mentor, and advisor assistance, as well as support from family and friends on a personal and professional level. These networks may provide moral support, useful guidance, and a sounding board for concepts and difficulties.

Continuous Learning: Harvard promotes an attitude of constant adaptability and learning. A balanced viewpoint and improved readiness to modify plans when necessary may be maintained by entrepreneurs by being receptive to new ideas and learning from both triumphs and setbacks.

Case Study: [Founder 13] and Their Approach to Work-Life Balance

Let's examine the life narrative of Emily, an HBS graduate who started WellnessWave, a company that offers comprehensive wellness solutions to people and companies, in order to highlight the concepts of work-life balance.

The Beginning: Emily founded WellnessWave as a result of her entrepreneurial spirit and love for wellbeing. The company's offerings included exercise plans, mental health resources, and wellness coaching with the goal of enhancing general wellbeing. As the company's creator, Emily had a strong sense of purpose and put in a lot of effort to start the company from the bottom up.

The Early Struggles: Emily had to deal with the typical obstacles of long hours and a lot of pressure in the early days of WellnessWave. She discovered that she was always working on the weekends and late into the night, often at the cost of her personal life. Emily had to reevaluate her strategy since the unrelenting pace was starting to negatively impact her relationships and health.

A Turning Point: Emily's attendance at an HBS work-life balance lecture, where she was taught the value of self-care and establishing boundaries, was a turning point in her life. Motivated by the realizations and resolved to discover a more healthful approach to managing her business, Emily made a decision to implement big adjustments.

Implementing Changes: Emily began by establishing distinct guidelines for her personal and professional lives. She reached a strict conclusion about her work and said that weekends were her only opportunity for personal leisure. Emily also started giving her team members greater authority over different parts of the company by giving them more responsibility. This reduced her burden and boosted the confidence and talents of her staff.

Making Self-Care a Priority: Emily made self-care a regular habit. She worked out and meditated in the mornings, which gave her body and mind clarity and energy for the day. In order to prevent burnout, she also made sure to take frequent breaks throughout the day. Emily discovered that she was more focused and productive at work when she put her health first.

Mindfulness Practices: Emily included mindfulness exercises for her staff as well as herself. She introduced mindfulness training once a week and pushed staff members to schedule self-care days. At WellnessWave, this promoted a positive and well-balanced work environment where everyone felt appreciated and cared for.

Flexible Work Arrangements: Emily implemented flexible work arrangements after realizing the variety of demands among her team. Workers have the option to work from home or modify their schedules to better accommodate their personal obligations. Because they felt trusted and empowered to handle their own schedules, team members' morale and productivity increased as a result of the flexibility.

Support Systems: More than ever, Emily depended on her support network. She engaged in peer groups with other entrepreneurs and often asked her HBS mentors for help. This network helped Emily through the highs and lows of her business career by offering insightful advice and supportive emotional support.

The Impact on WellnessWave: Emily's modifications had a significant effect on WellnessWave. With the help of a balanced and determined workforce, the business kept expanding and prospering. Consumers saw the company's dedication to health and positive culture, which matched its goals and core values. As a pioneer in all-encompassing health solutions, Wellness Waves standing grew, drawing in new business and collaborations.

Personal Growth and Satisfaction: Emily's personal growth and satisfaction were a result of attaining work-life balance. She found pleasure and a creative outlet when she reconnected with her hobbies outside of work, including hiking and painting. Emily took time to foster her ties with family and friends, which led to an improvement in those relationships.

Insights Learned: For businesses aiming to attain work-life balance, Emily's experience with WellnessWave provides insightful insights.

Set Boundaries: To keep work from invading every part of life, clearly define your personal time and work hours.

Delegate and Empower: To lessen your burden and promote a collaborative atmosphere, trust your team and assign responsibilities to them.

Make Self-Care a Priority: Include self-care activities in your daily routine to preserve your emotional and physical well-being.

Promote Flexibility: Offer adaptable work schedules to meet the demands of a wide variety of employees and to foster a positive workplace culture.

Seek Support: For guidance and inspiration,

rely on your professional and personal support systems.

Embrace Mindfulness: To reduce stress and maintain attention, practice mindfulness.

Final Thoughts

Finding balance between work and life is essential to becoming a successful business. It entails establishing limits, putting self-care first, and creating a welcoming and adaptable work atmosphere. Harvard Business School provides helpful advice on how entrepreneurs may successfully balance their personal and business lives without sacrificing one for the other.

Emily's experience with WellnessWave serves as a perfect example of how crucial balance is. Emily boosted her business and enhanced her personal life by consciously altering her attitude and putting her health first. Her experience serves as a reminder that business owners may succeed without sacrificing their well-being.

As you set out on your own business path, keep in mind that happiness and success over the long run depend on maintaining balance. Accepting the concepts of work-life balance can help you and your company find a fulfilling and long-lasting route. Greetings from the realm of balanced entrepreneurship, where business and well-being go hand in hand.

CHAPTER 15

CONTINUOUS LEARNING AND ADAPTATION

The Importance of Lifelong Learning

The path of entrepreneurship is marked by ongoing development and change. Long-term success in this changing context requires the capacity for constant learning and adaptation. Learning new things is just one aspect of lifelong learning; another is cultivating an innovative, growth-oriented attitude that welcomes inquiry. This entails improving abilities, keeping ahead of industry trends, and being receptive to fresh viewpoints and ideas for businesses.

The Changing Landscape: Global economic pressures, customer preferences, and technological innovations are the driving forces behind the constant evolution of the corporate environment. Entrepreneurs who make a commitment to lifelong learning will be better able to handle these developments. They are able to see new business possibilities, reduce risks, and make well-informed choices that advance their companies.

Adapting to Change: Lifelong learning naturally pairs well with adaptation. It entails being prepared to shift course as required, reconsider tactics, and put new policies into effect in light of evolving circumstances. Entrepreneurs who are successful know that holding onto outdated beliefs may impede advancement. Rather, they take a flexible attitude, prepared to change direction in the face of fresh facts and situations.

The growth mentality: The growth mentality, which holds that aptitude and intellect can be developed by commitment and effort, is the foundation of lifelong learning. A fixed mentality, on the other hand, is predicated on the idea that abilities are inherent and immutable. Growth-minded entrepreneurs are more tenacious, see obstacles as chances for improvement, and are less discouraged by failures.

Harvard's Culture of Continuous Improvement

Harvard Business School (HBS) has always supported lifelong learning and ongoing development. The values of rigorous analysis, practical application, and intellectual curiosity form the foundation of the institution's culture.

Students and graduates are imbued with these principles, which motivate them to strive for excellence in everything that they do.

Case Method: The case method of instruction is one of HBS's defining features. This method entails examining actual business situations, dissecting intricate problems, and talking about possible fixes. Students who use this approach develop their critical thinking skills, peer collaboration abilities, and ability to apply theoretical information to real-world scenarios. The case approach fosters a habit of ongoing investigation and introspection, which is necessary for lifetime learning.

Executive Education Programs: For seasoned professionals looking to further their expertise, HBS provides a selection of executive education courses. From finance and innovation to strategy and leadership, these programs cover a wide range of subjects. Through participation in these programs, entrepreneurs may ensure their continued competitiveness in their sectors by staying up-to-date on the newest trends and best practices.

Thought Leadership and Research: HBS faculty members are highly recognized for their contributions to business thought leadership and their research. Their work often tackles current issues and new prospects, offering entrepreneurs insightful information. Through regular attendance at HBS conferences, seminars, and publications, entrepreneurs may further deepen their awareness of pressing problems and creative solutions.

Alumni Network: A valuable asset for lifelong learning is the HBS alumni network. Alumni participate in talks, seminars, and activities on a regular basis to exchange information and advance their careers. This network offers a forum for idea sharing, experience sharing, and creating deep relationships that encourage ongoing development.

Case Study: [Founder 14] and Their Learning Journey

Let's look at the tale of Mark, an HBS alumnus who started GreenTech Innovations, a business focused on creating sustainable energy solutions, to demonstrate the value of ongoing learning and adaptation.

The Beginning: Mark set out on his adventure driven by a strong desire to have a good effect and a genuine enthusiasm for environmental sustainability. He started GreenTech Innovations with the goal of developing cutting-edge technologies that support renewable energy after earning his MBA at HBS. Initially, the firm concentrated on creating solar panels that were more cost-effective and efficient than those that were already on the market.

Early Success and Challenges: GreenTech Innovations' ground-breaking solar technology rapidly brought it acclaim. The business gained a devoted clientele and obtained many patents. But as the market for renewable energy developed, Mark saw that constant innovation and adaptation were necessary to maintain competitiveness. Keeping up with the quick changes in market dynamics and technology became a problem for him.

Embracing Lifelong Learning: Mark adopted the ideas of lifelong learning because he was committed to guiding his business to long-term success. He enrolled in HBS's executive education programs, where he studied leadership, strategic management, and advanced energy systems. He gained new insights and techniques from these seminars to help him deal with the challenges of the renewable energy industry.

Creating a Learning Culture: Mark saw how important it was to help his organization develop a culture of ongoing learning. He pushed his group to participate in knowledge-sharing exercises, go to industry conventions, and look for possibilities for professional growth. GreenTech Ideas organizes frequent internal seminars where staff members may discuss new ideas, exchange thoughts, and present their findings.

Adjusting to Market Developments: GreenTech Innovations encountered further difficulties as the renewable energy sector developed, such as heightened competition and altered regulations. Because of his dedication to learning and adapting, Mark was able to keep up with these developments. He started a calculated strategic turn to broaden the company's product line, going after wind energy and energy storage technologies.

Leveraging Technology: Acknowledging technology's capacity for transformation, Mark made investments in state-of-the-art instruments and systems to strengthen GreenTech Innovations' R&D capacities. The business used artificial intelligence to support predictive maintenance of energy systems and sophisticated data analytics to maximize product performance. These developments in technology have established GreenTech Innovations as a frontrunner in the sector.

Partnerships and cooperation: As part of his learning process, Mark also gave priority to partnerships and cooperation. To promote innovation and information sharing, he formed partnerships with academic institutions, governmental organizations, and other businesses. Through these partnerships, additional information, resources, and joint venture possibilities were made available.

Learning from Setbacks: There were obstacles along the way to achievement. GreenTech Innovations encountered many obstacles, such as disturbances in the supply chain and variations in the market. Mark, however, saw these failures as teaching moments. He carried out in-depth evaluations of every circumstance, saw opportunities for development, and put improvements into place to avoid similar problems in the future. The organization was able to increase resilience and flexibility because of this iterative methodology.

The Impact on GreenTech Innovations:

GreenTech Innovations greatly benefited from Mark's dedication to lifelong learning and adaptability. The firm achieved important milestones in the renewable energy industry while expanding and diversifying its product line. The innovative and exceptional reputation of GreenTech Innovations drew in new clients, financiers, and collaborators.

Personal Development and Fulfillment: Mark believed that lifelong learning went beyond achieving success in his career. Learning new things was a process that brought him satisfaction and personal progress. Mark's commitment to lifelong learning motivated his staff and fostered a culture of excellence and curiosity at work.

Takeaways: Mark's experience with GreenTech Innovations provides insightful takeaways for business owners:

Embrace Lifelong Learning: To keep ahead of industry trends and spur innovation, always seek out new information and abilities.

Cultivate a Learning Culture: To foster a culture of continuous improvement, support and encourage professional growth within your team.

Adapt to Change: Be prepared to change course and modify plans in reaction to new opportunities and changing market circumstances.

Leverage Technology: To improve capabilities and keep a competitive advantage, invest in cutting-edge technology.

Collaborate and Share Knowledge: Form alliances and work together with others to get access to fresh perspectives and materials.

Learn from Setbacks: See obstacles and disappointments as chances for development.

Final Thoughts

The path of an entrepreneur is characterized by constant learning and adjustment. To succeed over the long term and navigate the complexity of the corporate environment, one must embrace lifelong learning. The culture of continuous improvement at Harvard Business School offers insightful advice and practical tactics that keep business owners ahead of the curve.

Mark's experience with GreenTech Innovations is a prime example of how constant learning and adaptation can have a revolutionary effect. His dedication to learning new things, creating a culture of continuous improvement, and adjusting to changes made sure GreenTech Innovations stayed at the forefront of the renewable energy industry. The lesson from Mark's narrative is that learning and development are lifelong pursuits that are essential to both career and personal success.

As you pursue your business endeavors, never forget that learning never stops. Adopt the tenets of lifelong learning, maintain your curiosity, and have an open mind to fresh viewpoints. You will succeed in your company and improve your life with ongoing learning and development if you do this. Greetings from the realm of perpetual learning and adjustment, where achieving greatness is an endless quest.

CHAPTER 16

CREATING A LEGACY

Thinking Beyond Profits

The original motivation for starting a startup for many business owners is often centered on creative concepts, market disruption, and financial success. But as their endeavors expand, a deeper and more meaningful drive often surfaces: the desire to leave a lasting legacy. A legacy is more than just a successful business venture; it is about leaving behind something lasting that embodies the ideals and vision of the entrepreneur, impacts future generations, and has a significant social and cultural influence.

The Perspective Shift: When starting out, entrepreneurs prioritize growth and survival. The three most important things right now are getting capital, growing the business, and making money. But as the company expands and stabilizes, many entrepreneurs start to consider their wider influence. The process of creating a legacy begins when they begin to ask themselves questions such as, "What kind of company do I want to build?" and "How do I want to be remembered?" This change in viewpoint signals the start of the trip.

Creating Value Beyond Wealth: Leaving a legacy entails contributing to something more than just material prosperity. Contributions to the environment, industry, and community are all included. Beyond-profit entrepreneurs work to develop goods and services that enhance people's lives, promote sustainable behaviors, and effect positive change. They put a lot of effort into investing in social responsibility, emphasizing ethical behavior, and creating a workplace culture that reflects their beliefs.

The Role of Vision and Values: Having a strong vision and core values is essential to leaving a lasting legacy. The company's plans and actions are guided by the vision, which offers direction and purpose. As the moral compass, values mold the culture of the organization and have an impact on how business is done. Entrepreneurs that are successful in creating legacies instill their vision and beliefs in the foundation of their businesses, guaranteeing that these ideals will go on long beyond their own lives.

Harvard Perspectives on Making a Permanent Impression

The Harvard Business School (HBS) has a long history of developing executives who want to have a big, positive influence. Because of the school's focus on social responsibility, ethics, and leadership, entrepreneurs graduate with the skills and mentality necessary to leave lasting legacies.

Leadership with Purpose: According to HBS, effective leadership is about motivating and enabling people to realize a common goal rather than just running a business. Leaders that create lasting trajectories do it with a purpose, modeling their behavior and choices. Their objective transcends financial gain, as they aim to generate value for all parties involved.

Ethical Foundations: Integrity and ethics are essential components of HBS education. Entrepreneurs discover that acting morally is a tactical benefit as well as a legal need. Establishing a legacy calls for a steadfast dedication to moral behavior and the promotion of mutual respect and trust between staff, clients, and society at large.

Societal Responsibility: HBS urges business owners to think about their societal obligations. This entails being aware of how their corporate actions affect society and the environment more broadly. Entrepreneurs are instructed to follow environmentally friendly methods, assist neighborhood projects, and improve society as a whole.

Long-Term Thinking: Having a long-term outlook is necessary to have an effect that lasts. HBS places a strong emphasis on the value of strategic planning and vision. Entrepreneurs are urged to go beyond immediate profits and prioritize resilience, innovation, and sustainable growth. This long-term perspective contributes to the longevity of their legacy.

Inclusive development: Fostering inclusive

development is a crucial aspect of leaving a legacy. HBS promotes inclusivity and diversity because it understands that varied teams foster creativity and improve decision-making. Entrepreneurs are urged to establish welcoming workplaces where all people can thrive and contribute.

Case Study: [Founder 15] and Their Legacy

Let's examine the life of Sarah, an HBS alumni who started EcoPulse, a business committed to environmental sustainability and community development, to highlight the concept of leaving a legacy.

The Beginning: Sarah's journey started because she had a strong desire to protect the environment. She established EcoPulse with the goal of creating cutting-edge solutions for environmental problems after earning her MBA at Harvard Business School. The firm concentrated on developing environmentally friendly goods and innovations that supported sustainable living.

Early Vision and Values: Sarah's vision and values were evident from the beginning. She had an idea for a business that would lead the way in sustainability while also having a significant positive influence on the environment and local communities. Social responsibility, ethical business methods, and environmental care were among EcoPulse's basic ideals.

Innovative Products and Practices: EcoPulse made a name for itself fast with its eco-friendly appliances and biodegradable packaging. The business demonstrated its dedication to sustainability across its operations by implementing programs including carbon-neutral buildings and zero-waste production. These actions strengthened EcoPulse's standing as a pioneer in ecological sustainability.

Community Engagement: Sarah felt that contributing to the community was a necessary part of leaving a legacy. A number of community activities were started by EcoPulse, such as efforts to plant trees, environmental education programs, and assistance for regional conservation projects. These initiatives enhanced EcoPulse's reputation and bolstered client loyalty, in addition to helping the neighborhood.

Employee Empowerment: Sarah concentrated on fostering a positive and empowering work environment because she understood how important her staff members were to EcoPulse's success. The business established fair labor standards, offered chances for professional growth, and promoted an innovative and cooperative culture. Top talent was drawn to this welcoming atmosphere, which inspired workers to support the company's goals.

Ethical Leadership: Accountability, honesty, and integrity defined Sarah's style of leadership. Setting an exemplary example, she made moral choices even when they were difficult. Her dedication to morality won her the respect and confidence of stakeholders, clients, and staff, enhancing EcoPulse's standing as a business with high moral standards.

Sustainable Growth and Innovation: EcoPulse grew steadily and added more products while Sarah was in charge. The business kept up its innovative streak, spending money on R&D to produce cutting-edge sustainable products. By putting an emphasis on innovation, EcoPulse was able to stay ahead of the curve in business and promote good environmental effects.

Forging Partnerships: Sarah was aware of the influence that teamwork may have on producing long-lasting results. To strengthen its initiatives, EcoPulse collaborated with other businesses, nonprofit organizations, and governmental bodies. These collaborations allowed for the pooling of resources, the exchange of expertise, and cooperative projects that advanced EcoPulse's goals.

Legacy of Impact: EcoPulse's influence rose along with its size. Significant environmental gains have been made possible by the company's products and actions, which have reduced plastic waste and carbon emissions. With the help of EcoPulse's community activities, people and organizations were able to embrace sustainable practices, which had a good knock-on impact.

Personal satisfaction: For Sarah, creating EcoPulse brought her a sense of personal satisfaction in addition to professional success. Knowing that her business was changing the world gave her happiness and a sense of purpose. Her commitment to community service and sustainability inspired others and made a lasting mark on everyone she came into contact with via EcoPulse.

Takeaways: Sarah's experience with EcoPulse provides insightful takeaways for business owners hoping to leave a legacy:

Lead with Vision and Values: Clearly define the purpose and culture of your organization by establishing a set of core values.

Innovate for Impact: Concentrate on developing methods and products that promote constructive change and deal with social issues.

Involve with Communities: Actively support regional needs and issues by spearheading projects that enhance community well-being.

Empower Your Team: Create a welcoming and encouraging work atmosphere that enables staff members to support the goals of the organization.

Prioritize Integrity and Ethics: Make moral choices that foster respect and trust among stakeholders.

Think Long-Term: Make resilience and sustainable growth your top priorities when taking a long-term view.

Work Together for Greater Good: Form alliances that will multiply your efforts and have a wider effect.

Final Thoughts

One of the most significant and rewarding aspects of business is leaving a legacy. It entails looking beyond financial gain and concentrating on generating long-term value for the environment, society, and coming generations. The focus placed by Harvard Business School on social responsibility, ethics, and leadership offers a solid platform for business people hoping to leave a lasting impression.

Sarah's experience with EcoPulse serves as an excellent example of leaving a legacy. Her dedication to social responsibility, environmental sustainability, and moral leadership produced a business that was financially successful while also having a significant positive impact on the globe. Entrepreneurs are encouraged by Sarah's tale to lead with intention, innovate for impact, and leave enduring legacies.

Remember that the beliefs you maintain, the effects you create, and the people you touch will determine the legacy you leave behind as you pursue your business goals. Accepting the idea that there are more important things in life than making money can help you leave a lasting legacy that embodies your values, benefits your community, and motivates coming generations. Greetings from the road of creating a legacy, where your spirit of entrepreneurship creates a lasting impression on the globe.

CHAPTER 17

GUIDANCE FOR FUTURE BUSINESS OWNERS

Harvard Business Icons: Crucial Lessons

The path of business is a convoluted one, full of chances, difficulties, and life-changing lessons. The book features eighteen Harvard Business School (HBS) founders who have kindly shared their experiences, mistakes, and successes. Their combined experience provides priceless advice to anyone starting their own business. These Harvard Business Icons highlight the following important lessons:

Accept Failure as a Learning Opportunity: Failure is not the antithesis of success; rather, it is a component of it. Setbacks were faced by all of the founders, but they became stronger, learned from the experience, and adjusted. By seeing failure as a chance for personal development, roadblocks may become stepping stones.

Develop a growth mentality: A growth mentality is the conviction that aptitude and intellect can be enhanced by commitment and diligence. This way of thinking encourages flexibility and resilience. The founders constantly showed how overcoming obstacles and grasping opportunities require tenacity, curiosity, and a desire to learn.

Successful business people put a strong emphasis on adding value for their communities, workers, and clients. Their aim transcends financial gain; it is to address actual issues and have a constructive influence. This customer-focused strategy fosters loyalty and trust, which promotes long-term success.

Create a Strong Network: One of the most important tools for entrepreneurs is networking. The founders of HBS took advantage of opportunities, alliances, and mentoring via their networks. Creating and maintaining a strong network may provide connections, wisdom, and support that are essential for success.

Remain flexible and nimble: The corporate environment is ever-evolving, so being able to make quick decisions is crucial. The founders placed a strong emphasis on maintaining flexibility, being open to new ideas, and changing course as necessary. Entrepreneurs who are flexible may react to new possibilities and difficulties with effectiveness.

Lead with Integrity: The basis for creating a respectable and long-lasting company is integrity and ethical conduct. The founders continuously placed a high value on moral behavior, openness, and responsibility. Integrity in leadership cultivates respect and trust among stakeholders, which is essential for long-term success.

Invest in Your Staff: The effectiveness of a company's staff has a direct impact on its success. The founders emphasized the value of empowering employees and selecting bright, diverse candidates. Putting money into the training and welfare of employees boosts their morale and output.

Continually Innovate: The core of entrepreneurship is innovation. The founders promoted innovation and a culture of constant development. Maintaining a competitive edge and being up-to-date with emerging trends in the market may be achieved by your organization.

Useful Advice for Beginning Your Trip

Although embarking on an entrepreneurial path might be intimidating, prospective entrepreneurs can find guidance from the experiences of HBS founders. To get you started, consider these helpful pointers:

Begin with a Clear Vision: Specify your goals and objectives. Recognize your goals and the reasons for starting your own company. Your judgment and attention will remain focused on your objectives if you have a clear vision.

Do Extensive Market Research: To better understand your target market, competition, and industry trends, undertake extensive market research prior to launching. You'll be better able to see opportunities and make wise judgments with this information.

Create a robust business plan: A well-reasoned business plan explains your target market, value proposition, target company, revenue streams, and projected financials. It is essential for obtaining investment and acts as a blueprint for your company.

Start Small and Scale Gradually: To test your concept and get feedback, start with a minimal viable product (MVP). Utilize these suggestions to improve your offering and progressively expand your business. This strategy reduces risk and enables modifications in response to practical observations.

Create a Powerful Brand: Your brand is the impression that people have of your company, not simply your logo. Create a brand narrative that appeals to your target market. Building awareness and trust across all media requires consistent branding.

Emphasis on Customer Experience: Provide outstanding customer service to foster word-of-mouth and loyalty. Content clients are more inclined to stay with you and recommend you to others.

Obtain sufficient financing: Investigate a range of financing alternatives, such as crowdsourcing, venture capital, angel investing, and bootstrapping. Choose the one that best fits your company's demands and development goals, since each has advantages and disadvantages.

Leverage Technology: Make use of technology to improve productivity, expand your audience, and simplify operations. Your company may be greatly impacted by tools like social networking, e-commerce platforms, and customer relationship management (CRM) software.

Remain Strong: Being an entrepreneur is a journey, not a race. Remain strong in the face of difficulties and disappointments. Remain optimistic, take lessons from your mistakes, and keep moving ahead.

Seek Mentorship: Be in the company of mentors and advisers who can provide direction, encouragement, and insightful advice. Acquiring knowledge from seasoned business owners might help you steer clear of typical errors and accelerate your progress.

Inspirational Quotes from All 18 Founders

Here are some motivational statements from each of the 18 Harvard Business School founders that are included in this book to wrap up this chapter. Aspiring business owners might find inspiration and encouragement in these words of wisdom:

Founder 1: "Success is not final, failure is not fatal; it is the courage to continue that counts."

Founder 2: "Innovation distinguishes between a leader and a follower."

Founder 3: "Creating the future is the best way to predict it."

Founder 4: "Don't be afraid to give up the good to go for the great."

Founder 5: "You create opportunities; they don't just happen."

Founder 6: "Your time is limited, so don't waste it living someone else's life."

Founder 7: "Success usually comes to those who are too busy to be looking for it."

Founder 8: "If you are not willing to risk the usual, you will have to settle for the ordinary."

Founder 9: "The only place where success comes before work is in the dictionary."

Founder 10: "Do not be embarrassed by your failures; learn from them and start again."

Founder 11: "The road to success and the road to failure are almost exactly the same."

Founder 12: "I owe my success to having listened respectfully to the very best advice and then going away and doing the exact opposite."

Founder 13: "Would you like me to give you a formula for success? It's quite simple, really: double your rate of failure. You are thinking of failure as the enemy of success. But it isn't at all. You can be discouraged by failure or you can learn from it, so go ahead and make mistakes. Make all you can. Because remember, that's where you will find success."

Founder 14: "Success is not how high you have climbed, but how you make a positive difference to the world."

Founder 15: "Success seems to be connected with action. Successful people keep moving. They make mistakes, but they don't quit."

Founder 16: "The real test is not whether you avoid this failure, because you won't. It's whether you let it harden or shame you into inaction, or whether you learn from it; whether you choose to persevere."

Founder 17: The way to get started is to quit talking and begin doing," said **Founder 17**.

Founder 18: "Don't be distracted by criticism. Remember, the only taste of success some people get is to take a bite out of you."

Final Thoughts

Starting your own business is thrilling and difficult at the same time. The most important lessons from Harvard Business Icons are paired with helpful advice and motivational sayings to provide a thorough roadmap for following this route. Recall that being successful in business involves more than simply generating money; it also entails adding value, having a good influence, and leaving a lasting legacy.

Remember these tips when you go out into the realm of business for the first time. Accept failure, have a growth mentality, concentrate on adding value, establish solid networks, maintain your agility, lead with honesty, support your team, innovate constantly, and look for guidance. Your entrepreneurial path will be full of development, learning opportunities, and worthwhile achievements if you follow these guidelines.

Greetings from the entrepreneurial world. I hope the experiences of the Harvard Business School founders who have shared their knowledge with you in this book will inspire and influence you on your path.

CHAPTER 18

CONCLUSIONS AND PROSPECTS

The Future of Startups: What's Next?

The startup industry is always changing due to new developments in technology, altered customer behavior, and altered market dynamics. It's critical to investigate what the future holds for startups and entrepreneurs as we approach the dawn of a new age.

Technological Innovation: Cutting-edge technologies like blockchain, augmented reality (AR), artificial intelligence (AI), and the Internet of Things (IoT) will probably influence the next generation of businesses. These innovations will upend established markets in addition to opening up new ones. AI, for example, will transform businesses by allowing tailored consumer experiences, automating processes, and delivering deep insights via data analysis. Blockchain will improve transaction security and transparency, while augmented reality will change how customers engage with goods and services.

Sustainability and Social Impact: Sustainability and social responsibility are becoming more and more important to entrepreneurs. As consumers' awareness of social and environmental concerns grows, they anticipate that corporations will actively participate in finding solutions. Businesses that incorporate sustainable practices into their everyday operations—such as using environmentally friendly products or contributing to community projects—will not only satisfy customer needs but also foster greater brand loyalty. Furthermore, the popularity of "purpose-driven" company models emphasizes how crucial it is to strike a balance between profit and social effect.

Distributed Teams and Remote Work: The COVID-19 epidemic has hastened the spread of distributed teams and remote work, and this trend is here to stay. Future startups will adopt flexible work arrangements and remote work methods, using worldwide talent pools. It will become commonplace for entrepreneurs to work in distributed teams, necessitating the development of novel collaboration, communication, and team management techniques. Startups will be able to decrease overhead expenses and improve agility as a result of this change.

Health and Wellness: As people become more conscious of their physical and mental well-being, the health and wellness industry is expected to develop significantly. Startups will concentrate on cutting-edge solutions that support healthy living, such as telemedicine, mental health applications, and wearable fitness gear. The convergence of technology and wellness will open up new avenues for business owners to meet the changing demands of their clientele.

Personalization and Customer Experience: Hyper-personalization and outstanding customer experiences will define the startup landscape of the future. Businesses will be able to customize goods and services to each customer's tastes thanks to developments in AI and data analytics. Startups will have to make an investment to gain better knowledge of their clientele, using data to predict demands and provide tailored experiences. Developing enduring connections with clients will be a crucial point of differentiation in a cutthroat industry.

Diversity and Inclusion: Future businesses' success will be greatly influenced by diversity and inclusion. Diverse teams foster innovation and creativity by bringing in a variety of viewpoints and ideas. Employers will feel more a part of the company and attract top personnel if startups value diversity and cultivate inclusive environments. Furthermore, customers are supporting companies that more and more align with their beliefs, which makes diversity and inclusion a strategic need.

Harvard Entrepreneurship Predictions

The future of business and entrepreneurship has historically been shaped by Harvard Business School (HBS). Based on the perspectives of influential figures, scholars, and business specialists, the following are some significant forecasts for the future of entrepreneurship from Harvard:

Lifetime Learning Emphasis: Due to the rapid rate of change in the business world, entrepreneurs must possess a lifetime learning mindset. According to HBS, maintaining competitiveness would require ongoing education and skill development. To stay current with market trends and technological innovations, entrepreneurs will need to adopt new learning strategies, including online courses, micro-credentials, and experiential learning opportunities.

The notion of the "Entrepreneurial Ecosystem" is expected to become more widely recognized. These ecosystems, which include investors, colleges, government organizations, incubators, and accelerators, provide a conducive atmosphere for businesses to flourish. HBS predicts that these ecosystems will expand, encouraging information exchange, teamwork, and creativity among business owners.

Integration of Responsible and Ethical Practices: Corporate responsibility and ethical issues will be included in company plans. HBS places a strong emphasis on the value of moral leadership, openness, and responsibility in fostering stakeholder trust. To prosper in the long run, entrepreneurs will need to emphasize ethical business practices and negotiate difficult ethical problems.

Globalization and Cross-Border Collaboration: Entrepreneurship will become more and more international in the future. According to HBS, entrepreneurs will look for possibilities in developing economies and cooperate with foreign companies in order to grow outside local markets. As a result of globalization, businesspeople will need to establish international networks, negotiate legal frameworks, and comprehend a variety of cultural situations.

Impact of Digital Transformation: Startups will be at the forefront of this revolution as digital transformation continues to disrupt sectors. HBS emphasizes how crucial it is to use digital platforms and technologies to increase productivity, attract new clients, and develop creative company ideas. To be competitive, entrepreneurs will need to make technological investments and stay ahead of digital developments.

Emphasis on Mental Health and Well-Being: The importance of mental health and well-being will grow along with the demands of entrepreneurship. According to HBS, companies will put their founders' and workers' mental and emotional health first. A healthy entrepreneurial environment will need support mechanisms, including work-life balance programs and mental health services.

Shift Towards Decentralization: Future firms will be distinguished by their decentralized operations. According to HBS, blockchain-based business models and decentralized autonomous organizations (DAOs) that share decision-making authority among stakeholders will grow in popularity. This change will make entrepreneurship more accessible, enabling more people to start and profit from their own businesses.

Authors' Concluding Remarks

We, the writers, would like to leave you with a few parting thoughts and words of wisdom as we come to an end to our exploration of the world of business. The journey of an entrepreneur is paved with highs and lows, triumphs and setbacks, periods of uncertainty, and flashes of inspiration. It's a voyage that calls for fortitude, bravery, and unyielding resolve.

Cherish the trip: Being an entrepreneur is about more than simply getting where you're going; it's about appreciating the trip. Every obstacle you surmount, every accomplishment, and every lesson you pick up helps you develop as an entrepreneur. Have a cheerful outlook and an open mind as you embrace the adventure.

Remain True to Your Vision: Your vision serves as a beacon of hope and inspiration for you. Even when things become difficult, never waver from your goal. Others will be inspired by your enthusiasm and dedication to your goal, which will propel your company ahead.

Create Meaningful Relationships: The connections you make along the journey, with partners, customers, workers, or mentors, are priceless. Give these connections tender, loving attention and sincerity. Your business career may be significantly impacted by teamwork and outside assistance.

Embrace Change: Since the corporate environment is always changing, change is unavoidable. Accept change with flexibility and dexterity. Stay receptive to novel ideas, innovations, and chances that present themselves. Your success will mostly depend on your capacity for innovation and change.

Give Back to the Community: Remind yourself to give back to the community as you succeed. Future generations of entrepreneurs might be motivated and positively impacted by your efforts. Contributing to society, whether via social projects, charity, or mentoring, enhances your business legacy.

Believe in Yourself: The foundation of every successful business is self-belief. Have faith in your talents, follow your gut, and feel confident in the choices you make. Though there may be times when you question yourself, your self-belief will help you get through the difficulties.

Ongoing Education and Development: Becoming an entrepreneur is a lifelong learning process. Seek information constantly, go into uncharted territory, and want to advance both personally and professionally. You'll stay ahead of the curve and be ready for the future because of your dedication to learning.

Motivating Words from the Writers:

Eleanor Roosevelt once said, "The future belongs to those who believe in the beauty of their dreams."

"Success is not the key to happiness. Happiness is the key to success. If you love what you are doing, you will be successful." Schweitzer, Albert.

"The best way to predict the future is to invent it." Alan Kay, Jr.

"Your work is going to fill a large part of your life, and the only way to be truly satisfied is to do what you believe is great work. And the only way to do great work is to love what you do." Steve Jobs.

"Our doubts from today are the only thing preventing us from realizing tomorrow." Franklin D. Roosevelt

We are excited and full of hope as we consider the lessons imparted by the Harvard Business Icons and the direction that entrepreneurship is taking. The entrepreneurial spirit is a potent energy that spurs creativity, opens doors, and changes people's lives. We hope that this book's observations and anecdotes have motivated you, given you useful information, and stoked your enthusiasm for business.

For those who are prepared to take chances, dream big, and are dedicated to changing the world for the better, the future is bright. Remind yourself that you are not alone as you set out on your business adventure. You are a member of a dynamic and encouraging group of business owners who are changing the world.

We appreciate you coming along for the ride. We are excited to witness the amazing legacy you will leave behind and wish you the best of luck in everything that you do.

With appreciation and inspiration, The Writers.

CONCLUSION

Summary of Important Lessons

Let's pause for a minute as we finish this book and consider the adventure we've taken together. We have traveled over the vast terrain of entrepreneurship thanks to the tales, observations, and counsel of eighteen Harvard Business Icons. Every chapter has served as a springboard, guiding us closer to the core of what it means to be a profitable business owner. Let's go over a few of the most important things we discovered along the way.

The Startup Mindset: Chapter 1

We started off by investigating what the spirit of entrepreneurship is all about. Adopting an entrepreneurial mentality entails being resilient, flexible, and passionate about creating and innovating. The founders of Harvard Business School (HBS) instilled in us the significance of developing leadership skills and the worth of using failures as teaching opportunities.

Finding Your Niche: Chapter 2

Finding holes in the industry and using networks were emphasized as essential elements in building a solid company foundation. The founders of HBS shared their experiences to show how strategic positioning and astute market observation can lead to profitable niche discoveries.

Building a Sturdy Business Plan: Chapter 3

A startup's business strategy is its foundation. The need for a thorough strategy was emphasized, from outlining financial predictions to clearly identifying a value proposition. We discovered that thorough preparation might draw in prospective investors and open doors for effective implementation.

Obtaining Capital for Your Startup: Chapter 4

One of the hardest things about starting a company is getting financing. We looked at the many financing sources, such as venture capital and bootstrapping. Building a good case for investment and making a captivating presentation are critical components of recruiting investors, according to HBS insights.

Putting Together Your Ideal Team: Chapter 5

A startup's ability to succeed is closely linked to the caliber of its personnel. We discussed the significance of positive team chemistry and successful hiring practices. The founders of HBS discussed their experiences in developing teams that are not just competent but also in line with the mission and values of the business.

Product Development and Innovation: Chapter 6

Developing a concept from conception to market requires a thorough procedure. It was shown that innovation required constant work to keep one step ahead of the competition. The entrepreneurs' creative thinking and continual adjustments highlighted the process from idea to product launch.

Marketing and Branding: Chapter 7

Effective marketing techniques and a strong brand narrative are essential for drawing in new clients and keeping existing ones. The founders of HBS provided an example of how to use a variety of marketing media to establish a strong brand presence and construct narratives that connect with target audiences.

Scaling Your Business: Chapter 8

Growth has a unique set of difficulties. Growing pains were addressed, and strategies for sustainable growth were explored. The experiences of the founders made clear how crucial it is to continue operating efficiently and make adjustments for growing needs.

Chapter 9: Overcoming Obstacles and Setbacks

An entrepreneurial path is seldom without challenges. There was sharing of common hazards and failure-navigating techniques. The fortitude and success stories of the HBS founders taught us important lessons about tenacity and calculated turns.

The Function of Technology in Startups: Chapter 10

Technology is revolutionizing the startup environment. The use of technology to gain a competitive edge and the incorporation of tech solutions into corporate processes were stressed. The founders' tech-driven success served as a demonstration of innovation's transformational potential.

The World View in Chapter 11

Gaining a global perspective is necessary when venturing beyond local markets. We looked at ways to expand internationally and deal with different cultural environments. The worldwide endeavors of the HBS founders demonstrated how critical it is to comprehend and adjust to various market realities.

Ethical Entrepreneurship: Chapter 12

Long-term prosperity depends critically on morality and social responsibility. It was emphasized how crucial it is to engage in moral behavior and have a beneficial societal influence. The creators demonstrated how doing good may benefit business via their ethical business strategies.

Exit Strategies and Long-Term Vision: Chapter 13

Future planning includes thinking about both exit and scaling plans. Shared were insights on generating long-term value and exit strategies. The departure tales of the HBS founders provide a guide for organizing and carrying out a successful exit.

Work and Life Balance: Chapter 14

For long-term success, work and personal life must coexist together. We spoke about how to prioritize well-being and keep everything in balance. The founders placed a strong emphasis on the value of personal satisfaction and health in their approaches to work-life balance.

Chapter 15: Ongoing Education and Adjustment

Continuous development and lifelong learning are crucial in the quickly changing corporate environment. The founders' dedication to self-improvement and Harvard's culture of perpetual learning were highlighted as crucial elements in their success.

Building a Legacy: Chapter 16

Making a lasting impact is what entrepreneurship is all about, not just making money. There were shared insights on leaving a lasting legacy and changing the world for the better. The founders' heirlooms demonstrated how generational success in entrepreneurship is possible.

Chapter 17: Guidance for Future Business Owners

The combined experience of the HBS founders offered inspiration and useful advice for prospective business owners. A road map for starting an entrepreneurial journey was provided by the important lessons and motivational quotations, which included topics like accepting failure and using networks.

Motivation for Your Business Adventure

We want to send you a word of inspiration and encouragement as we wrap up this book. Although the path of entrepreneurship is not without difficulties, it is also replete with amazing prospects and benefits. You have the capacity to solve issues, develop something really amazing, and have a big influence on the world.

Believe in Yourself: Having confidence in oneself is the first and most important step in being an entrepreneur. Even in the face of difficulty, you will be motivated to go ahead by your self-assurance and vision. Recall that all successful business people began with a dream and the guts to follow it.

Acknowledge Failure as a Teaching Opportunity: Failure is an unavoidable aspect of being an entrepreneur. Instead of being afraid of failing, see it as an opportunity to grow. Every obstacle you face gives you the chance to improve, hone your strategy, and build resilience. The founders of HBS's experiences have taught us that failure is a necessary step on the road to success rather than the end.

Remain Agile and Adaptable: The corporate environment is ever-changing. Remain flexible and prepared to change course when called upon. Being agile enables you to react adaptably to novel possibilities and obstacles. Success or failure may depend on one's capacity for rapid adaptation.

Pay Attention to Value Creation: Creating value is the foundation of every successful company. Give your whole attention to addressing clients' requirements and fixing actual difficulties. Success comes easily when value creation is given top priority. Create goods and services that improve the lives of others.

Make Use of Your Network: Be in the company of peers, mentors, and advisers who are all there to help you. Make the most of these relationships to get chances, advice, and support. The founders of HBS have shown us the value of teamwork and networking in attaining success as entrepreneurs.

Dedication to Lifelong Learning: The path of entrepreneurship involves ongoing education and personal development. Remain observant, pursue knowledge, and remain receptive to new things. Make an investment in your career and personal growth. You will be more capable of navigating the challenges of entrepreneurship the more knowledge you acquire.

Make Ethics and Social Responsibility Your Top Priority: Manage your company with honesty and social responsibility. Building trust and loyalty among your stakeholders may be achieved through ethical practices and a dedication to creating a beneficial effect. The founders of HBS have shown that acting morally is not only the proper thing to do but also beneficial to business.

Establish Balance and Take Care of Yourself: Although being an entrepreneur might be hard, it's important to establish balance and look after your health. Make self-care a priority, and make sure your work-life balance is good. A robust physical and mental state are necessary for long-term success.

Remain Persistent and Passionate: The keys to success in entrepreneurship are perseverance and passion. Maintain your enthusiasm for your goal and persevere in the face of difficulties. Even in the face of challenges, your zeal and resolve will motivate others and keep you going ahead.

Leave a Legacy: Consider your legacy as well as your short- and long-term objectives. Make an effort to leave an impression that goes beyond your company. Whether it's via mentoring, social impact, or invention, your legacy will serve as a reminder of your entrepreneurial path.

Remember that you have the capacity to succeed when you set out on your business path. The ideas and anecdotes from the Harvard Business Icons serve as a monument to what can be accomplished when vision, zeal, and determination are combined.

Concluding Thoughts:

Simon Sinek once said, "Dream big, start small, but most of all, start."

"Success is not the result of spontaneous combustion. You must set yourself on fire." Arnold Glasow, Jr.

"The way to get started is to quit talking and begin doing." Disney, Walt

"Our doubts from today are the only thing preventing us from realizing tomorrow."
Franklin D. Roosevelt

We hope that this book has given you insightful knowledge, motivation, and useful advice for your path as an entrepreneur. Though there will be obstacles along the way, there are also many opportunities. Make an impact on the world, hold fast to your goal, and have faith in yourself. Your journey as an entrepreneur begins today, and we can't wait to see the amazing effect you will have.

We appreciate you coming along for the ride. Cheers to your accomplishments, development, and amazing legacy!

Warm regards, The Writers

www.ingramcontent.com/pod-product-compliance
Lightning Source LLC
Chambersburg PA
CBHW050049230526
45470CB00004B/1453